13 & COUNTiNG: *Does a Hamburger* Really Have *to Be Round?*

Engaging Activities to Foster Self-Esteem while Promoting Social Skills and Executive Function

by
TAMARA ZENTIC, M.S.

BOYS TOWN Press
Boys Town, Nebraska

13 & Counting: Does a Hamburger Really Have to Be Round?

ISBN 978-1-934490-83-9

Published by Boys Town Press
14100 Crawford St.
Boys Town, Nebraska 68010

Printed in the United States

10 9 8 7 6 5 4 3 2 1

For a Boys Town Press catalog, call 1-800-282-6657
or visit our website: BoysTownPress.org

Boys Town Press is the publishing division of Boys Town, a national organization serving children and families.

Table of Contents

Why Is the Topic of Self-Esteem Important?

The effects of low self-esteem can be debilitating for youth. Low self-esteem can have a negative impact on every aspect of a youth's life. This book is meant to offer strategies and activities that assist in building confidence in students and bringing about a healthier awareness of identity-related issues.

The "Does a Hamburger Really Have to Be Round?" lessons are coupled with the Boys Town Education Model®, which promotes the use of life skills and behavior training through the implementation of Boys Town social skills. The lessons also invite and encourage the use of Executive Function Processes as part of the teaching emphasis. Executive Function Processes include qualities like zest, curiosity, social intelligence, and self-control, to name a few.

Keeping in mind the developmental level of 5th- to 12th-grade students, "Does a Hamburger Really Have to Be Round?" provides easy-to-implement, effective strategies to help improve self-esteem and foster healthy identity perspectives. The lessons are time-effective and relational, and get to the heart of the issues. They give youth the opportunity to explore their values, beliefs, and ways of thinking. Furthermore, there is an emphasis on incorporating the use of technology, through various devices, into the lessons to better engage and motivate the students of the digital 21st century.

How Will Your Students Benefit from This Book?

- Students continually struggle with their identity and various self-esteem issues. These lessons help to combat negative thinking and stereotypes that surround these challenges.
- It's a great way to incorporate Boys Town social skills into a topic that affects each one of your students.
- The activities are developmentally appropriate for 5th- to 12th-graders.
- The lessons elicit thought-provoking discussions and self-examination.

- The activities are easy to use and don't require a large amount of prep time.
- Technology is widely used to engage and motivate students.
- This book can be used in numerous settings such as the classroom and homeroom, and in advisement, enrichment, interventions, and character programs.

How to Use this Activity Book

Using the activities and lessons in "Does a Hamburger Really Have to Be Round?" is a great way to help youth learn about and explore self-esteem issues they face. The lessons have been structured so they can be taught in a class period, or can be extended and approached in ways that spread the lesson over two or three class times. Lesson length often will be dependent upon the amount of discussion that is generated in the classroom.

Each activity provides a "Materials List" and step-by-step "Instructions" on how to deliver the lessons. These provide structure but give teachers flexibility to tailor activities for each class of unique learners and the issues they are facing. Boys Town social skills are woven throughout the lessons and activities, as well as through the "Executive Function Objectives." There also are suggestions for how to deliver the content in a "flipped classroom" approach. Detailed, teacher-friendly instructions help teachers feel at ease when implementing the lessons that require a broader use of technology. Finally, because helping teachers conserve time is a priority, additional resources are listed, along with suggested answers to discussion questions.

Introduction

"Who am I?" is a question or at least a thought that most, if not all, of us have had at some point in our life. It is natural for a person to wonder about his or her feelings, values, beliefs, and purpose for existing. All of us have examined the ways we behave, our perspectives on life, and the inner workings of our mind on more than one occasion.

For some, finding an answer to this age-old question is ever-elusive. Many get a glimpse of who they are but never fully uncover their true identity, while others seem to grasp their purpose, who they are, and who they are becoming with a sense of ease and inner confidence. Why is this? What is the difference? Why do some people struggle incessantly and others peacefully glide?

Let me introduce you to one of Zane's stories. Zane is a typical college-age student who is usually looking for a way to make some money. The dollars run short for a boy with an appetite. Fortunately, he has a pretty sweet deal working three or four times a year for a company that sells sporting merchandise at our nation's major sporting events, including the Final Four, the Super Bowl, the College World Series, and major college football bowl games. Zane loves working for this company! The company not only pays him a very healthy wage, but also provides his food and lodging while he is working, which is typically for a week or two. Sound like a job you would like? Me too! For Zane, there is only one drawback. He doesn't always get to pick the type of food provided for each meal. Sometimes, it is sandwiches or a hot meal; other times, it's just a salad. One thing you should know about Zane is that he is a VERY selective eater. We don't use the "v" word (vegetables) or the "f" (fruits) word around him too often. On this particular day, it was "Salad Day" at the College World Series. This is where his story picks up….

"It was Salad Day and let me start off by saying how much I HATE salads. I mean, come

on, get me some real food; some MEAT! If I wanted to eat leaves in a bowl, there are plenty of trees around to make it happen. So, naturally, I said 'No way' to the salad and decided I would use my break to go get some other 'edible' food for myself. As it turns out, there was a hot dog stand not too far away. I thought, 'Perfect! I'll go get a couple of dogs!' I walked up to the stand and realized they also had BURGERS. Now, I LOVE – let me repeat myself – I LOVE a good burger! So I ordered two. My mouth was watering with anticipation as I waited for my food. I could almost taste the juicy, delicious, savory, flavor of BEEF! My stomach was starting to growl and gurgle when I saw the worker approaching me with my food. He placed the basket on the table and left. My eyes darted to my food in sweet anticipation of the big, fat, round, juicy burgers, but… to my utter shock and horror, I found two hotdog buns in the basket. They had given me hot dogs? No wait! They were burgers – in a hot dog bun! No wait! They were burgers, shaped like hot dogs, in hot dog buns! What?!?!?!?!?!?!?! Was this some type of cruel joke? What was happening?

"At first I was skeptical. Then I was just downright scared to eat them. If they were crazy enough to serve burgers in the shape of a hot dog, on hot dog buns, well, then they were pretty much capable of anything, if you know what I mean.

"I examined the meat and buns carefully. Finally, after what seemed like an eternity, I got so hungry that I bravely took my first nibble. 'Wait a minute!' I then took a very large bite! This was the BEST-TASTING BURGER I HAD EVER EATEN!

"In one nibble and one bite, my whole perception of a 'Burger' had changed. I was eating the most delicious burger ever, yet it was in the shape of a hot dog. It was not what I had expected and has forever changed the way I think about and view my food. I have decided that if we get caught up in judging the way our food looks, we might just miss out on the 'Best-Tasting Burger' in the world."

It is easy to relate Zane's story to people as well. We look at people with anticipation. We expect them to think and act in certain ways. We are disappointed when they fall short of our expectations. We judge them by their looks and what they have to offer us. Like a hamburger, we expect them to be "round" and served on a "round" bun. We are taken back when someone does not fit the "mold."

The question becomes, "Why?" Why are we confused or taken back when someone does not fit our "mold" of who they should be or what they should look like? Weren't we all made the way we were intended to be? Why are we so quick to point out each other's faults and imperfections? Do we focus on the notion that someone has the wrong "shape," or that they don't have enough "seasoning"?

No two people were created to be the same. Each of us is slightly different from everybody else. We are UNIQUE! We were made to be different. Just as when we get caught up in judging the way our food looks, and might possibly miss out on the "Best-Tasting Burger" in the world, we also can get caught up in judging others (and in turn, criticizing or bullying them) and miss out on something valuable they have to offer us. If we can accept others and ourselves for who we are and what we look like, then we will be on our way to "peacefully gliding." Then our self-esteem will possess the inner confidence that eludes so many of us.

So let me ask you, "Does a Hamburger really have to be Round and fit the 'mold' in order to be great?"

We know what the message is; now let's tap into the minds of our youth and become "Somebody's Difference!"

SECTION 1

Defining Self-Esteem

The adolescent years are a time of rapid change. Not only does a youth's appearance change, but also their abilities. On top of this, the way they think and feel goes through a series of fluctuations on a consistent basis. During these years of growth and development, youth are searching for their own unique identity. They want to be part of a group, yet they also want to set themselves apart based on their own special abilities, talents, and attributes.

For these reasons, this becomes a critical time for promoting positive, healthy, self-esteem in our young people. In order to be the best they can be and achieve their goals and dreams, they must have the resources to help them build a healthy view and appreciation of themselves. However, before they can begin this process, they need to better understand what self-esteem really is and be able to honestly evaluate the self-esteem they currently possess in order to start moving forward. The following lessons are designed to help students analyze, understand, and evaluate where they currently fall on the self-esteem scale.

Lessons in this section include:

- **?!? Self-Esteem ?!?**
- **Positive or Negative?**
- **Quotes on Self-Esteem**
- **Who Are You?**

?!? Self-Esteem ?!?

OBJECTIVES:

Social Skills: While participating in the activity, students will practice their skill of "Talking with Others," while using the skill of "Staying on Task."

Executive Function: Students will show zest by actively participating and show self-control by paying attention and resisting distractions. Actively listening to others will demonstrate curiosity.

MATERIALS NEEDED:

- Paper for the "Class Interest Board"
- Sign or banner with the "Kids Health" quote (see Step 2)
- Paper
- Pencils
- Paper for "pins"
- Markers
- Staples, push pins, or magnets for pinning
- Poster of the Boys Town social skill, "Talking With Others"
- Poster of the Boys Town social skill, "Staying on Task"

TEACHER NOTE:

Self-esteem is what we think of ourselves. It is those little conversations we have in our head about how much value we have. It is the judgments we make about the qualities, attributes, or abilities we possess. Defining our self-esteem means we have to knowingly or unknowingly give our self a number on society's self-esteem scale.

TEACHER INSTRUCTIONS:

1. Make a "pin it" self-esteem board. Title it "Class Interest Board" and write in many headings, such as "Self-Esteem," "Boundaries," "Definitions," "Self-Image," etc. Put the board in an area of the room where you can utilize it for a good portion of the school year.

TIPS

You could reuse this "Class Interest Board" for many of the lessons in this book!

2. Have students read the following quote from the **Kids Health** website (www.kidshealth.org) and write their answer to the question at the end on a piece of paper:

> "You can't touch it, but it affects how you feel. You can't see it, but it might be there when you look at yourself in the mirror. You can't hear it, but it's there when you talk about yourself or when you think about yourself! What is this important but mysterious thing?"

3. Ask for volunteers to share their answers. Explore several answers but eventually get students to the answer: self-esteem.

4. Next, direct the students to get into groups of two or three and come up with a group definition of what self-esteem is. Before the students begin working, take the time to instruct them on how to **talk with others** when doing group work, and appropriate ways to participate in the activity:

    a. Look at the person you are talking to.
    b. Use a pleasant voice.
    c. Include others by asking questions.
    d. Don't interrupt when someone else is talking.

5. Discuss each skill step, as appropriate.
Along with this, remind students of the importance of **staying on task**:

   a. Look at the task and think about the steps needed to complete it.
   b. Focus all your attention on the task.
   c. Stop working only when given permission by the adult who gave you the task.
   d. Ignore distractions and interruptions by others.

6. When they have written their group definition, ask the students to share their ideas with the class. Talk about each definition.

7. Direct students to "pin" their definitions to the "Class Interest Board." (Explain how many people use Pinterest and "pin" ideas, messages, lessons, fashion, etc. to their own boards.) Explain to students that they will be adding to the "Class Interest Board" during other activities throughout the school year as they learn more about self- esteem.

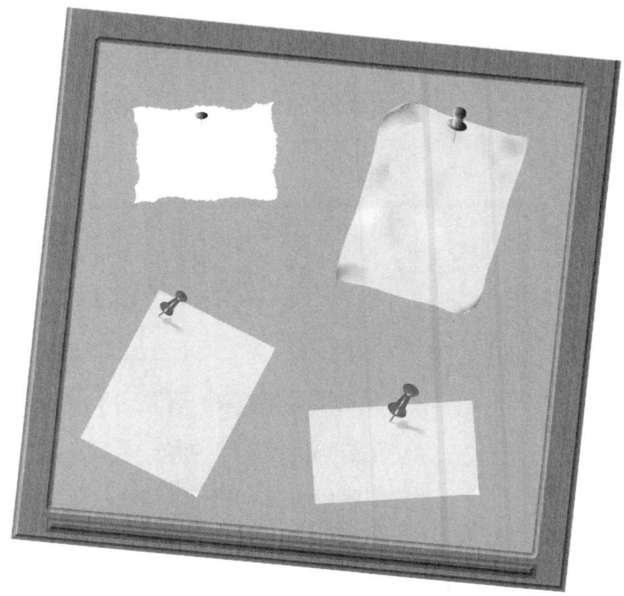

TIPS

Plan for several "pins" when constructing the Board. You could also make your own "pin board" for your class on Pinterest.

FLIPPED CLASSROOM:

Have students explore online sites that can help them become familiar with how people create a "pin it" board. Students could also come to class with their own definition of self-esteem and then begin the group work.

ADDITIONAL RESOURCES:

Search through books or online to become more familiar with self-esteem. Visit online "pin" sites to become more familiar with how the board should work.

Positive or Negative?

OBJECTIVES:

Social Skills: Students will spend time assessing their own talents and abilities and identifying their feelings concerning this assessment.

Executive Function: Students will exhibit some form of curiosity as they seek to understand their own self-esteem.

MATERIALS NEEDED:

- "Self-Esteem Scale" handout
- Paper
- Pencils
- Phone camera or iPad
- T-chart (with a "Positive" column and a "Negative" column)
- Class T-chart
- Poster of the Boys Town social skill, "Assessing Own Abilities"
- Poster of the Boys Town social skill, "Identifying Own Feelings"

TEACHER NOTE:

If an individual has positive, healthy self-esteem, she won't feel the need to tell others how good she is. She is simply okay with who she is. Individuals with high self-esteem see their own good traits but also recognize that they have some weaknesses, but are okay with that. Students with lower self-esteem will oftentimes try hard to gain approval or attention. They are unsure of themselves and many times have a difficult time seeing their strengths as well as their weaknesses. A student with low self-esteem may feel like he is "stuck" and will always be "stuck."

TIPS

Many good self-esteem scales can be found online. For this lesson, you can either use the very simple one we have included or find one on the Internet (for example, the Rosenberg Self-Esteem Scale, which includes a scoring system within the scale).

TEACHER INSTRUCTIONS:

1. Hand out a "Self-Esteem Scale" to each student and have them complete it.

2. Remind the students that their "Self-Esteem Scale" will be private so they should answer the questions very honestly. Ask the students to **assess their own abilities** using the following guidelines:

    a. Make a list of your strengths and weaknesses.
    b. List examples of when you have been successful or have had problems.
    c. Think about future activities where you could use your abilities.

3. After the students have completed the "Self-Esteem Scale," give them a copy of a blank T-chart. Ask students to use the T-chart to think about themselves as well as their classmates and how they would look and act if they had positive self-esteem. Have them record their thoughts on the "Positive" side of the chart. Then have the students think about how they and their classmates would look and act if they didn't have positive self-esteem, and record those thoughts on the "Negative" side of the chart. (For example: doesn't brag, is friendly, and is positive about school and life would go on the "Positive" side, and things like quits, avoids, is controlling or aggressive, bullies, lies, denies, and tries to be the class clown would go on the "Negative" side.)

4. Once the students have completed their individual charts, compile all the answers on a class T-chart.

5. Ask students to express their feelings about their own self-esteem and list 8 to 10 of their responses on each side (positive/negative) of the class T-chart. It may be easier for students to come up with the negative ideas, but it is important that they also see that they have just as many good qualities. Have them use the following strategies for **identifying their feelings**:

    a. Examine how you are currently feeling.
    b. List and think about how your feelings change with different situations and experiences.

c. Think about how you could monitor your feelings and emotions when situations occur.
d. Correctly identify and label your feelings.
e. List your feelings.

Discuss these steps, and ask the students to write on their "Self-Esteem Scales" whether they have more positive or negative self-esteem.

6. Have each student use an iPad or camera phone to take a "selfie" (a picture of themselves) that they think represents their current level of self-esteem. Ask them to save the photo onto a computer and send you a copy. You can either keep these private or post them on the "Class Interest Board." After the class has completed all the activities in this book, have the students take another "selfie" and compare the two photos. Share the two different pictures with the class at that time and "pin" them to the "Class Interest Board." (Selfies send the message that "**I am free to be me**!")

Prior to this activity, ask the students to bring their iPads or phones that have cameras to class with them. Make arrangements for students who don't have these devices to take a photo of themselves. Be sensitive to students who suffer from low self-esteem; they may have more difficulty filling out the "Self-Esteem Scale" and the T-charts. It would also be helpful for you to compile a list of negative and positive self-esteem qualities before beginning this activity.

FLIPPED CLASSROOM:

Ask students to interview other people or find resources on the Internet about the difference between low and high self-esteem. Have them make a T-chart of 7 to 10 examples of both before coming to class. The class can then spend more time creating a group list and completing the "Self-Esteem Scale," giving them more time to reflect on their own self-esteem.

ADDITIONAL RESOURCES

Self-esteem scales found online

NAME:________________________

DATE:________________

ACTIVITY

Self-Esteem Scale

DIRECTIONS: Please read each statement and decide whether you agree or disagree with what it says. Check the appropriate column. Hand your paper to the teacher when you are finished.

STATEMENT	AGREE	DISAGREE
1. I am good at most things I do.		
2. I mess up a lot.		
3. I feel like I'm a part of a fun group of friends.		
4. I usually have a good attitude about my abilities.		
5. It really bothers me if someone criticizes me or my work.		
6. I don't think most people even know I'm here.		
7. I feel good about myself.		
8. I am not happy with the way I look.		
9. I don't feel like there is anything very good about me.		
10. I am proud of my abilities and accomplishments.		

Quotes on Self-Esteem

OBJECTIVES:

Social Skills: Students will practice making positive self-statements.

Executive Function: Students will show participation and effort as they get started, pay attention, and finish their work.

MATERIALS NEEDED:

- Visual (e.g., poster) of quotes on self-esteem
- Poster papers (11"x17")
- Markers, crayons, or colored pencils
- Booklet paper
- 3-hole punch for booklet
- Poster of the Boys Town social skill, "Making Positive Self-Statements"

TEACHER INSTRUCTIONS:

1. Two to three days before this lesson, ask the students to bring five quotes on self-esteem to class. The quotes can be from either a positive or a negative viewpoint. Tell them to make sure they write down the source of the quote (students can use people, online sources, books, etc.).

2. Prior to the lesson find several quotes on positive and negative self-esteem. Have these as a back-up for students who do not bring any to class and/or do not have access to the Internet.

3. In class, ask students to share some of their quotes with the group. Then have them select one or two of their favorites, rewrite the quotes on a piece of booklet paper, and include their name somewhere in their quotes to make them personal.

4. Remind each student to write his or her own self-esteem quote based on his or her own experiences. Stress the importance of **making these positive "self" statements**:

   a. Make a positive statement about an actual occurrence or accomplishment.
   b. Don't lie or exaggerate. Be honest!
   c. Say to yourself, "I'm proud of…" or "I think I did well or better at...."
   d. Remember not to brag or put others down.

5. Collect the students' papers and make a class booklet of all the quotes, which students can refer to over the course of the school year.

6. Give each student a piece of poster paper. Ask students to design and color a cartoon character for the favorite quote they wrote on the booklet paper, and to write that quote on the poster paper with a marker. When all the students have finished, have them hang their posters on their lockers. (If your school has a policy that does not allow hanging things in the hallways, hang the posters around your classroom or in a designated commons area in the school.)

TIPS

Have extra self-esteem quotes available for students who don't bring any to class.

FLIPPED CLASSROOM

Have students interview five people at random and ask them for their definition of self-esteem, both good and bad. Have the students bring the answers they get to class and start this lesson at Step 3.

ADDITIONAL RESOURCES:

Numerous quotes are available online.

Self-Esteem Quotations

"Wanting to be someone else is a waste of the person you are."

– *Marilyn Monroe*

"My best friend is the one who brings out the best in me."

– *Henry Ford*

"The better you feel about yourself, the less you feel the need to show off!"

– *Robert Hand*

"No one can make you feel inferior without your consent."

– *Eleanor Roosevelt*

Who Are You?

OBJECTIVES:

Social Skills: Students will analyze tasks and stay on task.

Executive Function: Students will exhibit grit by working independently with focus.

MATERIALS NEEDED:

- "Who Are You?" silhouette template worksheet
- Paper
- Pencils
- Construction paper in various colors
- Markers, colored pencils, crayons
- Poster of the Boys Town social skill, "Analyzing Tasks"
- Poster of the Boys Town social skill, "Staying on Task"

TEACHER INSTRUCTIONS:

1. Explain to students that at this point, they may be starting to recognize they are good at some things, okay at some things, and not so good at others. Stress that this is normal and okay! Tell them no one can be great at everything. We can, however, accept ourselves as we are and choose to focus, through education and hard work (otherwise known as "grit"), on certain areas to become more well-rounded. Explain to students that every person has his or her own specific traits, abilities, and talents. Some are easily recognized and some take longer to uncover. Furthermore, some will not be developed until later in life.

2. Review with students how to **stay on task** before starting the project:

    a. Look at the assignment.
    b. Think about the steps you will need to follow.
    c. Focus all your attention on the task.
    d. Stop working only when given permission by the adult who gave the task.
    e. Ignore distractions and interruptions by others.

3. Also instruct students in **how to analyze the tasks** to be completed:

   a. Ask questions to clarify the assignment, if necessary.
   b. List the steps of the task.
   c. Put the steps in order.
   d. Begin completing the steps in order.

4. Tell the students they will be constructing an illustration of their good, okay, and not-so-good traits, abilities, and talents. Have students choose one of the following options and follow the instructions:

   a. On the premade "Who Are You?" silhouette template, draw and color activities that represent traits, abilities, and talents you feel you have in each of the three categories: good at, okay at, not so good at. Color the silhouette and cut it out.
   b. On a free online photo collage site, such as www.ribbet.com, register for a free account. Using your own file or Facebook photos or ones from a website, pick a format for the photos and arrange them in the three categories (traits, abilities, talents) as a collage. Give your login information for your collage to the teacher. (For easier access, the teacher could make one teacher account and have all the students who choose this option work under that one account.)

5. After students complete their project, ask them to write one to three paragraphs explaining the representation of their traits, abilities, and talents. Have them include what they are good at, okay at, and not so good at. They also could include how they feel about those areas. For example, are they okay with not being good at some activities?; What could they do about it?; How does this affect their self-esteem?

6. Post the paragraphs with the silhouettes or the collages.

TIPS

Research a photo collage site ahead of time and make sure you can get a free account. You can construct a collage about yourself and then show it to the students as an example. You also might have to help some students identify areas in which they think they possess good abilities, talents, or traits.

FLIPPED CLASSROOM:

Have the students make a photo collage of themselves at home or outside of class. When they come to class, have them write their paragraphs and present their work.

ADDITIONAL RESOURCES:

Various online photo collage sites; online templates of silhouettes

NAME:______________________________

DATE:________________

ACTIVITY

Who Are You?

DIRECTIONS: On the template below, draw and color activities, traits, or abilities that you feel you have in each of the three categories: Good At; Okay At; Not So Good At. When you have finished drawing/coloring your person, write one paragraph on each section on the back, telling what the section represented. What are you good at, or not good at? What are your feeling about these areas?

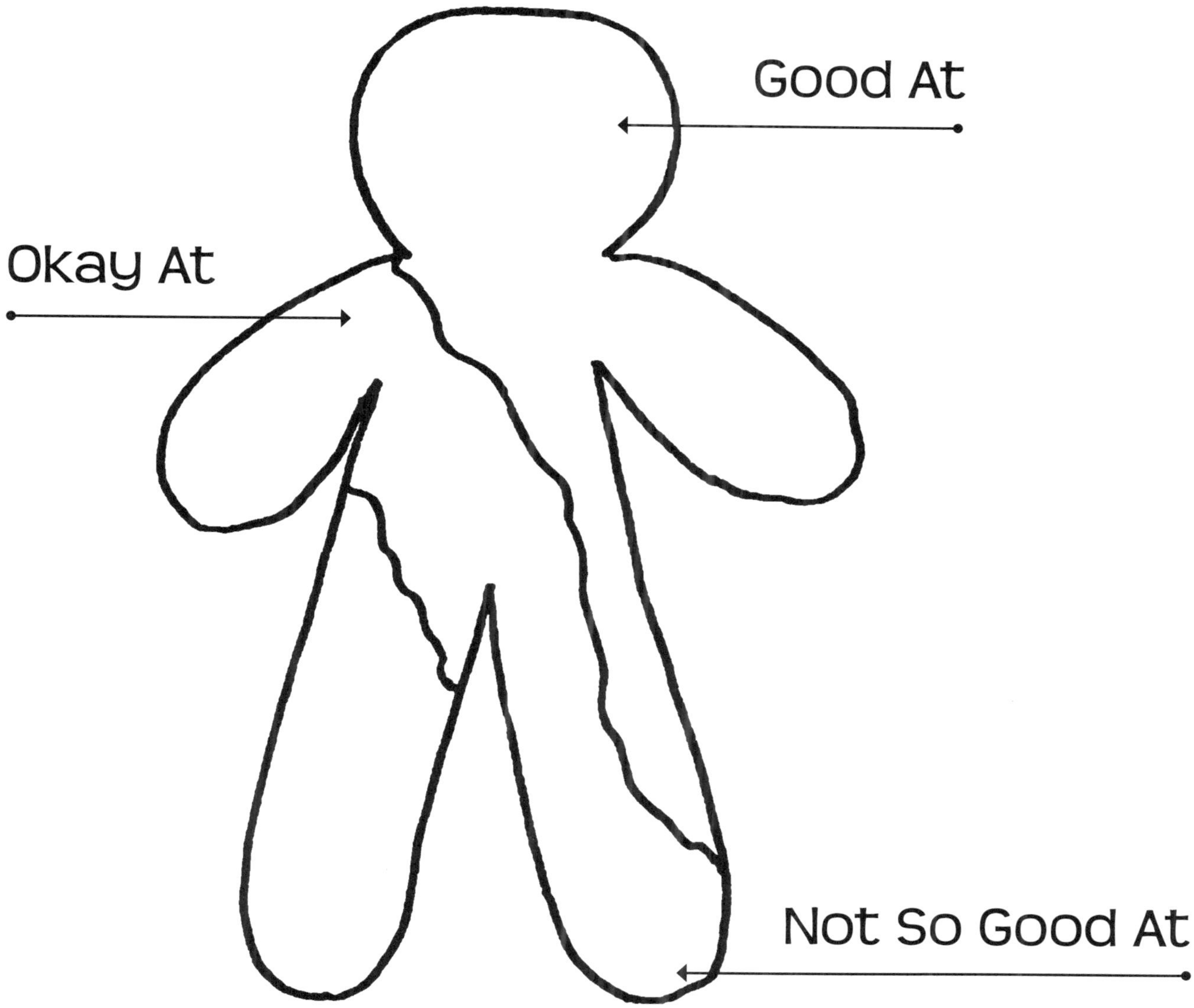

(continued)

Answer the following questions in complete sentences.

1. Are you okay with not being good in ALL areas?

2. What could you do about it?

3. How does it affect your self-esteem?

SECTION 2

How We Got Here

When one speaks of self-esteem, many listeners automatically associate the word with appearance, and more specifically, with body image. Others think of popularity. These two areas can affect self-esteem, but beauty, or the lack thereof, in terms of physical appearance is not what self-esteem is all about. I think my sister-in-law has it right when she says, **"Beauty is as beauty does!"** It is NOT about what you look like but rather about how you act and influence others. Good, healthy self-esteem can't find a solid foundation if it is built on shaky, fleeting, and sometimes shallow premises. People learn self-esteem; they are not born with it.

Having positive self-esteem means having an appreciation for **ALL** of oneself, even one's shortcomings. When people can appreciate and value all the areas of their lives that make them unique – their mind, intellect, emotions, abilities, and relationships – then self-esteem increases.

We should all try to be the best WE can be and realize that we have just as much value as a person, individually as well collectively, as someone who has reached society's exceptional standards. **Self-esteem is being okay with who you are even though you're not perfect.**

Lessons in this section include:

- **So, DOES a Burger Really Have to Be Round?**
- **Can You See It?**
- **Positively Unique!**
- **My Esteem or Your Esteem?**

So, DOES a Burger Really Have to Be Round?

OBJECTIVES:

Social Skills: Students will explore appropriate ways to contribute to a discussion.

Executive Functions: Students will pursue grit by working independently with focus.

MATERIALS NEEDED:

- Paper
- Pencils
- "Does a Hamburger Really Have to Be Round?" story
- "Don't Judge a Book" worksheet
- Colored pencils, crayons
- Poster of the Boys Town social skill, "Contributing to Discussions"

TEACHER INSTRUCTIONS:

1. Ask the students to describe, in their own words on a piece of paper, what a hamburger looks like. Emphasize using descriptive adjectives and remembering to state the color, shape, and texture. Ask them to draw a quick picture of what the burger would look like.

2. Have students share their descriptions. Point out the shapes of the hamburgers the students drew. Most, if not all, will have drawn the burger in a circular shape.

3. Read the first part of the story, "Does a Hamburger Really Have to Be Round?," to the students. Show them the picture of what Zane's burger actually looked like. **Read only the first portion of the story, stopping before the meaning of the story is discussed.**

4. Ask the students for their reactions to the story.

5. Ask students how this story relates to self-esteem. (Possible answers: Sometimes we think we have to look a certain way in order to be accepted; If we don't look just right, it can affect our self-esteem and make us feel insecure; Self-esteem is often tied to how people view their body.) Then read the remainder of the story that covers its meaning.

6. Before asking the following questions, take time to review how students should appropriately **contribute to a discussion**.

   a. Look at the people who are talking.
   b. Wait for a point when no one else is talking.
   c. Make a short, appropriate comment that relates to the topic.
   d. Choose words that will not be offensive or confusing to others.
   e. Give others a chance to speak.

7. Ask the questions below and discuss the students' answers as a class. Or, if you prefer to have small group discussions, hand out the "Don't Judge a Book" worksheet and have students discuss the same questions in small groups. (Be certain to walk around during small-group discussions. Because the topic is sensitive, conversations can be emotional.)

   a. What do you say about the way you should look?
   b. What do your peers say about the way you should look? (Discuss trends kids are currently following.)
   c. What does culture say about the way you should look? (Touch on the pressure kids face to look a certain way that is often portrayed in the media.)
   d. Can we become too critical about the way we look?
   e. Can self-criticism ever be a good thing?
   f. How do we know the difference between healthy feedback and unhealthy criticism?
   g. Do you think you have ever missed out on a possible friendship with someone who could have been "a best-tasting burger" because that person didn't look like you thought he or she should?

8. Challenge students to compose one-sentence reminders you can post in the classroom that will challenge them to accept people for how they are and to look for their hidden good qualities instead of focusing on their external appearance. (Example: **"Be YOUR Best and Forget the Rest!"**)

TIPS

This may become a sensitive subject for some students. Approach it with compassion and empathy.

NAME:______________________________

DATE:______________

ACTIVITY

Don’t Judge a Book Worksheet

DIRECTIONS: In small groups, answer and discuss the questions below. Be prepared to also discuss them as a class.

1. What do you say about the way you should look?

2. What do your peers say about the way you should look?

3. What does culture say about the way you should look?

4. Can we become too critical about the way we look?

5. Can self-criticism ever be a good thing?

6. How do we know the difference between healthy feedback and unhealthy criticism?

7. Do you think you have ever missed out on a possible friendship with someone who could have been “a best-tasting burger” because that person didn’t look like you thought he or she should?

Can You See It?

OBJECTIVES:

Social Skills: Students will apply strategies to display effort during the activities.

Executive Functions: Students will practice self-control by paying attention and resisting distractions.

MATERIALS NEEDED:

- Images of fictitious characters your class will recognize (see suggestions at the end of this lesson)
- Cardstock or laminator
- White board or chalk board
- Paper
- Pencil
- Images of famous people in with and without their disguises (see suggestions at the end of this lesson)
- Poster of the Boys Town social skill, "Displaying Effort"

TEACHER INSTRUCTIONS:

1. Prior to class, pick several fictitious characters with whom students would be familiar and print off an image of each one. Glue or laminate the images to cardstock. Randomly number them and display them on a countertop. You will also need to have the images of famous people in disguises and without disguises ready to show the students.

2. Review the expectations for **displaying effort** on the lesson activities:

   a. Remain on task and work diligently.
   b. Do your best to accomplish tasks to criteria.
   c. Inform others of your efforts if appropriate.

3. Ask students to view each fictitious character and rank them from best to worst, with the best being the character with the highest self-esteem and the worst being the character with the lowest self-esteem. Students also must write down a reason for each of their rankings.

4. Discuss the rankings as a class. On the board, list the reasons the students give for their rankings of the characters.

5. Explain to the students that these were characters they probably were familiar with, but now you are going to shift the focus. On the board, write: "Do you think you can recognize a person who has a good body image and self-esteem just by looking at him or her? If so, what signs do you look for? If not, why?" Let students share their answers.

6. Show the students the images of famous people you have selected in disguises. Don't tell the students who they are, but have them rate each person's self-esteem on a scale of 1 to 10, with 10 being the highest. Ask students to share their reasons for the ratings.

7. Reveal the identity of the famous people by showing the images of them without their disguises. Have students re-rate the self-esteem of the famous people, again giving reasons for their ratings.

8. Ask the following questions:

   a. Can you determine the level of a person's self-esteem based on what he or she looks like?
      (Answer: No)
   b. Why do we judge people by their looks?
      (Possible answer: As a society, we value beauty.)
   c. Should we let other people's opinions of how we look bother us? How do we keep from doing this?
      (Possible answer: No, focus on ourselves.)
   d. Besides appearance, what are other things upon which we should base a person's value?
      (Possible answers: personality, character, work ethic, etc.)
   e. What beliefs do you hold about yourself? About others?

Have all your images prepared or bookmarked before starting the lesson.

FLIPPED CLASSROOM:

At home, have students find the images of 7 to 10 fictitious characters and rank them from best self-esteem to worst self-esteem. Have them write down the reasons for their choices. Have students bring their images, rankings, and reasons to class.

ADDITIONAL RESOURCES:

Websites with images of fictitious characters, famous people in disguise, and famous people. The following celebrities have some interesting disguises: Dr. Adolph Brown (speaker); Mel Gibson (Mr. Cool Disguise); and Kim Kardashian.

List of some possible fictitious characters: Batman, Snow White, Shrek, Scrooge, Superwoman, the Aladdin Genie, Waldo, Wizard of Oz characters, Harry Potter, Barbie, Spiderman, the Joker, Winnie the Pooh, Mario, Snuffleupagus, RoboCop

Positively Unique!

OBJECTIVES:

Social Skills: Students will assess their own abilities.

Executive Functions: Students will discover they possess gratitude as they evaluate their abilities.

MATERIALS NEEDED:

- Access to computer
- "Positively Unique" worksheet
- Colored paper
- Glue sticks
- Paper
- Pencils
- Chalk board or white board
- Poster of the Boys Town social skill, "Assessing Own Abilities"

TEACHER NOTE:

Self-esteem is more than just body image or how an individual feels about his or her appearance. Self-worth is influenced and shaped by our minds (thoughts and intellect), our emotions, our values, and our relationships with other people. It is important for students to recognize their uniqueness and how they can develop higher self-esteem by appreciating their own abilities and talents.

TEACHER INSTRUCTIONS:

1. Remind students that although body image affects our self-esteem, our appearance is not what our self-esteem should be based on!

2. As a class, have students brainstorm other things that can either increase or decrease a person's self-esteem. Make a list of the students' suggestions on the board. Most of their suggestions should fall under four main categories:

   a. Mind/Intellect
   b. Emotions
   c. Abilities/Talents
   d. Relationships with Others

   Discuss these categories with students, as appropriate.

3. Hand out the "Positively Unique" worksheet to students. Ask them to list 10 things about themselves for each category. This may be difficult for some students but it is essential that they begin to recognize the many good qualities that make them unique. **Assessing one's own abilities** requires one to:

   a. Make a list of your strengths and weaknesses.
   b. List examples of when you have been successful or have had problems.
   c. Think about future activities where you could use your abilities.

4. Have students use their "Positively Unique" worksheet to create a work cloud or word art using an online program such as Tagxedo or Wordle. You could also use an online program for this part of the activity.

5. Print the students' completed work cloud or word art projects and have the students mount them on a piece of colored paper. Display the projects in the classroom.

TIPS

You might need to help students think of their positive traits.
Plan ahead for students to use computers.

FLIPPED CLASSROOM:

Assign students to ask five people, outside of class, what they believe influences the formation of a person's self-esteem. Have the students use the responses they receive to create a small word cloud or word art on Wordle or Tagxedo and bring it to class. After they have made a small word cloud or word art in class, they could compare the two.

ADDITIONAL RESOURCES:

Other word cloud or word art programs

NAME:____________________________________

DATE:____________________

ACTIVITY

Positively Unique

DIRECTIONS: Please list 10 good qualities you have in each category. In the last column select the 3 qualities you think are your best and write them in that space.

	My Mind	My Emotions	My Abilities	My Relationships	My 3 Best Qualities
1					1
2					
3					
4					2
5					
6					
7					3
8					
9					
10					

My Esteem or Your Esteem?

OBJECTIVES:

Social Skills: Students will identify and write down a goal of their choice.

Executive Functions: Students will display optimism by believing that effort will improve their future. Students will develop more grit in their life by trying very hard to reach their goal.

MATERIALS NEEDED:

- Examples of "Personal Records" (PRs)
- Visual of the "Author Unknown" quote in Step 1
- Paper
- Pencils
- Poster of the Boys Town social skill, "Setting Goals"

TEACHER NOTE:

Whether we are aware of it or not, we constantly compare ourselves to others, whether it be our abilities, our looks, and how much money we have. Society says that the more and the better we have, the more value we have; this puts pressure on us to try harder or to do things like artificially improving our looks. But whatever happened to "just being yourself"? Shouldn't we have the same amount of value because we are who we are, regardless of where we fall on the societal scale of value? Is it a healthy practice to compare ourselves to others? This lesson is designed to get students to view themselves apart from others and to judge only their own growth in comparison to their own self.

TEACHER INSTRUCTIONS:

1. Show students the visual of the following quote: **"The only person you should try to be better than is the person you were yesterday." Author Unknown.** Discuss the meaning of this quote.

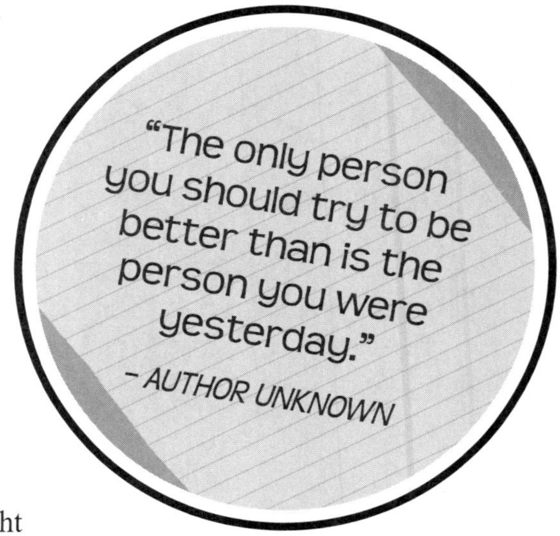

2. Ask students if they know what a PR or PB is (Personal Record and Personal Best). Some students will have heard of these, but others probably will have not. So explain to them that these acronyms are often used in athletics. For example, track athletes go for a PR or PB in their event, which means they are trying to improve their own time or record, not necessarily beat the other competitors. Ask students why they think coaches might use PRs and PBs with their athletes.

3. Instruct students to think of an activity they have performed and write it down on a piece of paper. Using that activity, have them **set a new goal** following these strategies:

a. Decide on an overall value and lifestyle desire.
b. Identify the resources you need to meet these.
c. List the steps needed to meet your goal.
d. Establish short- and long-term goals that will help you meet these steps.

4. Explain to the students that when they reach their goal, they will have set a new Personal Best or Personal Record. **When we compare ourselves to only ourselves, we base our self-esteem on the only thing we have control over – ourselves.** And we don't have to worry about not measuring up to someone else's Personal Record or Personal Best.

5. Give students time to practice reaching their goal or setting a PR or PB. Have them sign and date the goal they wrote down when they accomplish it and their PR.

6. Ask students the following questions:

   a. Why do you compare yourself to others? (Possible answer: Somebody else gets more attention.)
   b. What usually happens when we compare? (Possible answer: Anxious and negative thoughts.)
   c. Is this a good habit or not? (Answer: No.)
   d. What is a better way to improve your self-esteem? (Possible answer: To work only on myself.)

TIPS

Help students set reasonable goals. The goals themselves don't matter as much as the student working toward them in order to improve themselves.

SECTION 3

The World Around Us

Values shape who we are. They give us our individuality. Values are subjective, based on each individual's viewpoint in life; therefore, an individual's viewpoint and values make him or her unique.

Values create our moral compass. They provide us with a set of guidelines for our life. When our values align with the values of those around us, our self-esteem is affirmed and we feel a part of the group. This makes us feel good about ourselves because we feel that we are being true to our values and lifestyle. If our values do not agree with those around us, then there is conflict. We experience inner turmoil that can lead us to feel that we are not being true to ourselves, therefore lowering our self-esteem.

The more important our values are to us, the more they will affect our self-esteem. Take, for example, someone who strives to place equal value on family time and time spent with friends, but finds he is spending far more time with his friends. This conflict of values can produce feelings of guilt, resentment, and inadequacy in the family, thus lowering self-esteem.

Furthermore, if individuals value and possess those qualities that society values – hard work, helping others, citizenship, having recognition, to name a few – then they cultivate a higher sense of self-worth because they are aligned with their culture.

Lessons in this section include:

- **What Message Do We See?**
- **Digital ID & Self-Esteem**
- **Social Media & Self-Esteem**
- **Values**
- **To Teach Another**

What Message Do We See?

OBJECTIVES:

Social Skills: Students will analyze social situations that affect self-esteem. They will demonstrate hard work by persevering on the assignment.

Executive Function: Students will practice self-control by allowing others to speak without interrupting. They will deepen their understanding through curiosity by asking and answering questions.

MATERIALS NEEDED:

- Articles from newspapers, magazines, or online
- Paper
- Pencils
- "Article Response Questions" handout
- Poster of the Boys Town social skill, "Analyzing Social Situations"
- Poster of the Boys Town social skill, "Persevering on Tasks and Projects"

TEACHER INSTRUCTIONS:

1. Bring several newspaper articles to class for the students to review. You also could use articles you find online or in a magazine.

2. Ask the students to pick an article about somebody in the news. Have them critique whether the article was written in a positive light about the person, or in a negative light. Have them support their answer with examples from the article. This will require students to **analyze the social situation**. Remind students of the steps:

    a. Think about the people you encountered.
    b. Look at the situation.

c. Assess the behaviors of others.
d. Choose the behavior or reaction that seems most appropriate.

3. After they've analyzed the articles, instruct students to think about what one article's message could do to the self-esteem of the person whom the article was about.

4. Have the students form small groups (two or three students) and share their thoughts on the article and the message they think it sends to the person it was written about. Remind students that they will get better results if they **work hard on the task**. To do this, they should:

   a. Know what must be done.
   b. Get started promptly without procrastinating.
   c. Remain on task until finished.
   d. Deal appropriately with any frustrations.

5. Ask each group to compile a list of words or phrases from the article that could promote low self-esteem and ones that could promote higher self-esteem.

6. Next, have each group write a response to the person the article was written about concerning these self-esteem issues. Have students consider the following questions (post these questions on a flipchart or make copies of the "Article Response Questions" handout and give one to each student or small group):

   a. Should the person care about what was being written?
   b. Does it mean he or she is really that kind of person?
   c. Is the person really that bad, or good?
   d. What if something totally opposite was written about him or her the next week?
   e. Should someone base his or her self-esteem on what someone else says or writes about him or her? Why or why not?
   f. How would you feel if this article had been written about you?

7. Ask students to discuss how this activity lesson could relate to them. Do they base their self-esteem on what someone else does or doesn't say about them? Could this change next week? Are they really what other people say they are? The point is to have students recognize that they can allow their own self-esteem to drop because of what their peers say or do, and to understand this is not a good habit.

8. "Pin" some of the students' responses from Step 6 to the "Class Interest Board" that was created in Lesson 1.

TIPS

Have some articles already selected for groups that might struggle to find one. Emphasize how this activity relates to their social world.

FLIPPED CLASSROOM:

Have students gather examples of how famous people or people in the news deal with positive and negative comments and bring them to class.

ADDITIONAL RESOURCES:

Online articles about people in the news or famous people

NAME:______________________________

DATE:________________

ACTIVITY

Article Response Questions

DIRECTIONS: Use the questions below to help create a written response to the subject of the article you were assigned.

1. Should the person care about what was being written? ____________________

2. Does it mean he or she is really that kind of person? ____________________

3. Is the person really *that* bad, or good? ____________________

4. What if something totally opposite was written about him or her the next week?

5. Should someone base his or her self-esteem on what someone else says or writes about him or her? Why or why not?

6. How would you feel if this article had been written about you?________________

Digital ID & Self-Esteem

OBJECTIVES:

Social Skills: Students will engage in self-monitoring and reflection techniques. They will also practice setting boundaries.

Executive Function: Students will obtain an informal assessment of their social intelligence by understanding how others can influence their digital ID.

MATERIALS NEEDED:

- Digital communication devices (phones, computers, iPads, etc.)
- Little cards for "tips" (can be index cards or 4"x6" pieces of paper)
- Poster paper
- Paper
- Pencils
- "Setting Boundaries" handout
- Poster of the Boys Town social skill, "Self-Monitoring and Reflection"
- Poster of the Boys Town social skill, "Setting Appropriate Personal Boundaries"

TEACHER NOTE:

Our youth are vulnerable to self-esteem issues at school and at home, as well as through their interactions involving digital communication devices. Properly educating students about these devices helps protect their self-esteem in these areas.

TEACHER INSTRUCTIONS:

1. Poll the students on what type of digital communication devices they use on a regular basis. Post the results for the class to see. (Avoid identifying devices by specific student names; instead just give the types of devices students commonly use.) Use a free online or digital poll app or a simple type of traditional, in-class poll.

2. Have each student use one of the types of digital communication devices they mentioned to text or email the following questions to 5 to 10 people: "Is your Digital ID or self-esteem different or separate from your regular self-esteem?" Have students share the responses they receive without naming those who responded.

3. Ask students the following questions:

    a. What is your Digital ID? (Possible answer: Who a person is on a digital device. These devices can record important facts and information about a person. A person's identity is matched with the digital world.)
    b. Who are you in a digital setting? Does this differ from who you are at school or at home?
    c. Do you believe a Digital ID is a permanent recording of who you are or can it be erased or deleted?

TEACHER NOTE:

You are trying to help students understand that their Digital ID is unique to them. It is probably safe to say that everyone has some form of a Digital ID, but it is not as private as students believe it is. Their digital activity can track what they do, what sites they visit, what calls they make, or what texts they send. So, if they are acting one way or trying to create a separate Digital Identity through their devices, they need to know it will likely be linked to their own identity and self-esteem.

4. Ask students to keep track of their digital communication activity for one day. Ask them to be specific (for example, who did a text go to or who was one received from? How long did they use each device?).

5. At the next class, have students share the amount of time they spent on each device. (Again, be careful not to single individuals out.)

6. Ask the students to **reflect on what they discovered about themselves (self-monitoring and reflection)**. Remind students to:

a. Think about the behaviors you are engaging in and your feelings about this.
b. Label these behaviors and feelings.
c. Determine whether they are appropriate.
d. Identify alternate behaviors or skills that would be more productive.

Have students record their responses to these steps on a piece of paper.

7. Based on the fact that our digital activity can be traced, coupled with the amount of time youth are spending on these devices, ask students if they see any problems or dangers associated with this in terms of their safety and their self-esteem.

TEACHER NOTE:

Help students understand these points – what they think is private is not; self-esteem can be easily damaged on digital devices because some individuals will say things online or by text that they would not say in person; looks and identities can be masked; others have access to personal information that could compromise their safety.

TIPS

Make a list of your own ideas about this prior to the discussion.

8. With these things in mind, ask each student to write down five ways he or she could protect his or her self-esteem and safety while using digital devices. On a piece of poster paper or on the board, create a group list of the students' suggestions. Be sure to include the following ideas:

a. Use privacy settings on photos.
b. Ask others to remove photos of people they have tagged.
c. Search my name and see what comes up. Take steps to eliminate any negative messages or photos.
d. Manage my sites thoughtfully and carefully.
e. Never post while angry.
f. Think Before You Act!
g. Set boundaries.

9. Pass the "Setting Boundaries" handout out to students. Read the steps for **setting boundaries** to students, and instruct them to visualize the following:

   a. Imagine a series of circles radiating out from you. Each represents a boundary.
   b. Picture people you know or encounter in various circles, according to the relationship you have with them.
   c. Disclose personal information only to those in your closest circle.
   d. Touch others only in ways that are appropriate to your relationship with them and to your boundaries.

10. Have students write down two or three personal boundaries they will set within each of the circles.

11. Ask students to choose any suggestions from the list you made and have them create a tip sheet for teens on how to protect their self-esteem while using electronic (digital) devices.

TIPS

You could type these tips on little cards and distribute them to other students in the school.

12. Finally, inform students that if they are in a crisis or just distressed by a negative digital experience, they can and should tell a trusted adult. There are steps that can be taken to help.

TIPS

It would be helpful to show as many examples of negative digital experiences as possible. Try to maintain anonymity on examples and suggestions. Become familiar with various electronic devices before beginning this activity.

FLIPPED CLASSROOM:

Have students research the pros and cons of digital devices when it comes to self-esteem. Ask them to be specific and give at least 10 examples.

ADDITIONAL RESOURCES:

There are many online resources for Internet safety, such as www.ic3.gov, that you can use as resources.

NAME:______________________________

DATE:______________

HANDOUT

Setting Boundaries

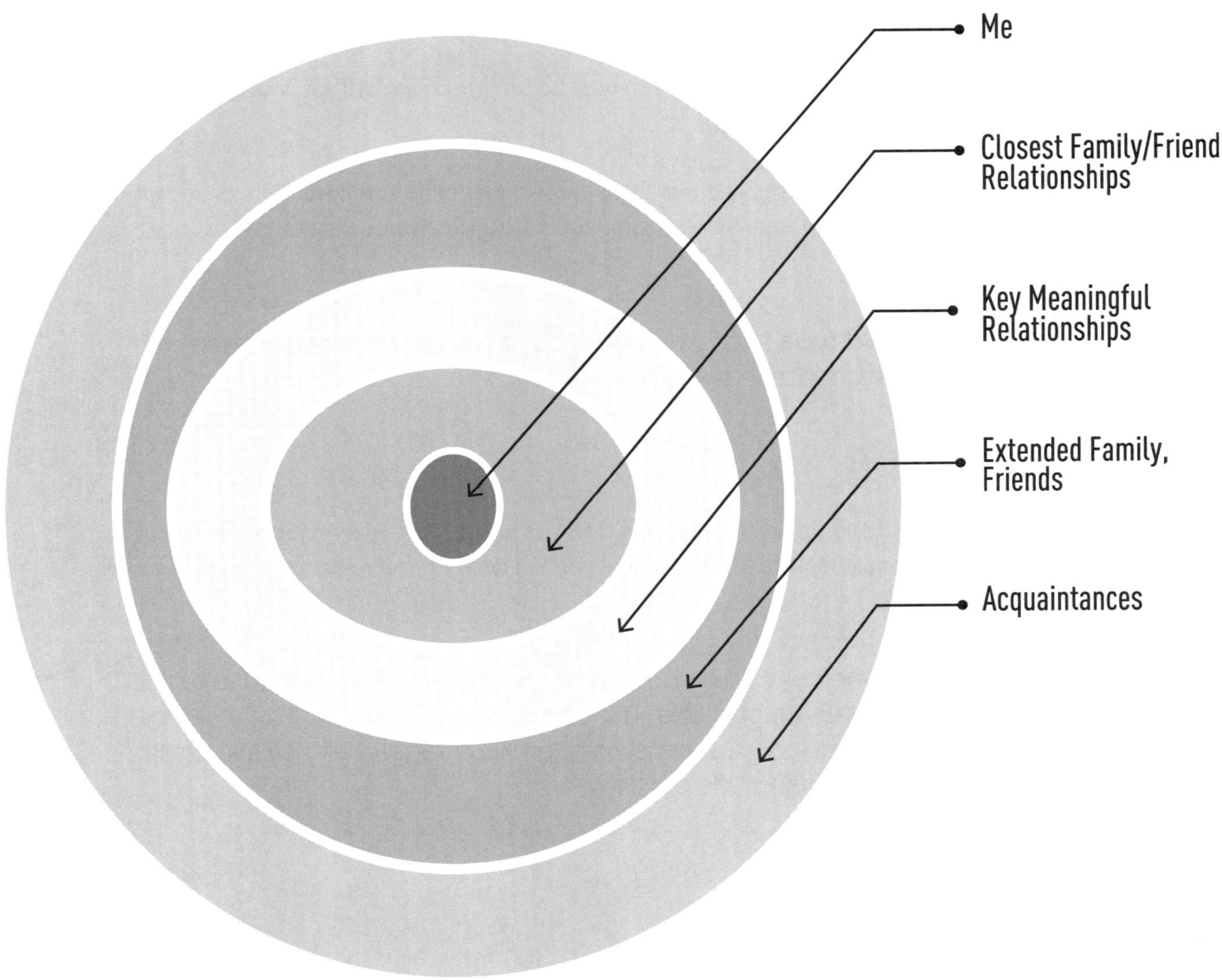

Social Media & Self-Esteem

OBJECTIVES:

Social Skills: Students will cooperatively gather information.

Executive Functions: Students will practice self-control by paying attention, resisting distractions, and following instructions. They will utilize organizational skills while doing surveys to gather information.

MATERIALS NEEDED:

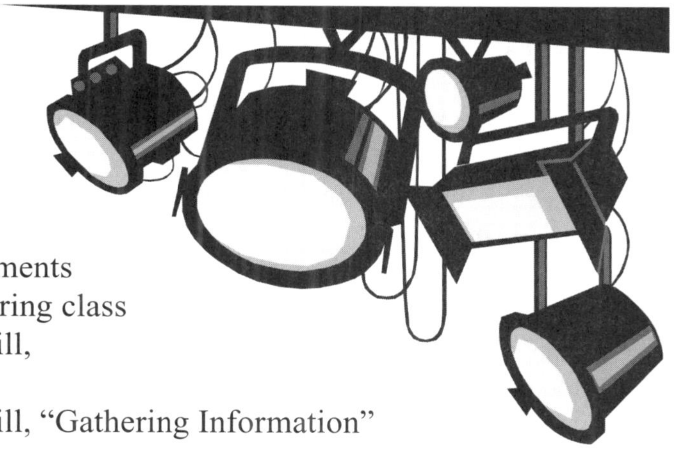

- Paper
- Pencils
- Access to the school intercom system or message system
- "Social Media" worksheet
- Sample Public Service Announcements (PSAs) for students to preview during class
- Poster of the Boys Town social skill, "Cooperating With Others"
- Poster of the Boys Town social skill, "Gathering Information"

TEACHER NOTE:

Once students have identified the relationship between their Digital ID and their self-esteem (in the previous lesson), it will be easier for them to determine how social media can play a part in shaping their self-esteem.

TEACHER INSTRUCTIONS:

1. Write the following questions on pieces of paper and post them around the classroom.

   a. What is a social media site? (Possible answers: There are several good definitions on the Internet; www.familystoriesblog.com states that a "social media site is a place on the Internet where people share information, interact and communicate with each other. " Facebook, Twitter, etc.)
   b. Why do youth like social media?
   c. Why do youth visit these sites?
   d. Which sites do you prefer or are teen favorites?
   e. Do you think adults prefer other sites or the same ones?
   f. Describe one social media site for me.
   g. List all the social media sites you visit.

2. Have students discuss each of these statements and questions as a class.

3. Hand out a "Social Media" worksheet to each student and have students complete them.

4. As a class, have the students create a survey based on the questions posted around the room and those on the "Social Media" worksheet.

5. Have the class break into smaller groups, and have each group use the survey to interview each of the following people outside of class: an elementary school student, a middle school student, a high school student, a college student, an adult, and a senior citizen.

6. Remind students to use the following social skills to complete this activity.

   To **cooperate with others,** they should:
   a. Discuss the task with others.
   b. Know what to do.
   c. Give constructive criticism to and accept it from peers.
   d. Share resources.
   e. Praise peers' efforts.

   When **gathering information** for their surveys, they should:
   a. Know their topic by researching the topic further.
   b. Ask for help if needed.
   c. Assemble the surveys.
   d. Write down the results as they gather them.

TEACHER NOTE:

Some students will need assistance in organizing this task and recording their answers.

7. When the students return to class after completing their survey interviews, have the groups compile and discuss their results.

8. Using the information from this activity, have each student group create a "Spotlight School Message" based on social media and self-esteem. This should be similar to what we call a Public Service Announcement (PSA), and it should be short and to the point.

TIPS: Have students review your examples of PSAs to see how they are designed.

9. Ask the school principal for permission to have the students read one "Spotlight School Message" each day over the school intercom. They also could post their messages on the class or school website. (Make sure you edit the messages before they are read or posted.)

TIPS: When doing research to prepare for this activity, save some PSAs on your Web browser "favorites" to show students. Become familiar with several social media sites prior to this activity.

FLIPPED CLASSROOM:

Ask each student to survey the following people on their own outside of class, using the questions from the activity: elementary student, middle school student, high school student, college student, adult, and senior citizen. They can do this online or in person. Have students compile the results, bring them to class to discuss, and use them to create their "Spotlight School Message."

NAME: ANSWER KEY

DATE: ______

ACTIVITY

Social Media Worksheet

1. What can occur on social media sites that can affect a person's self-esteem?

Safety issues, bullying, addictions, gossip, mean and hateful words, intimidation, etc

2. How can social media improve a person's self-esteem?

Healthy communication between people can give a person confidence and boost self-worth, people can share common interests, etc.

3. How can a person's self-esteem be damaged by social media?

Users can degrade, bully, or make fun of someone, spread rumors, not "friend" people, etc.

Values

OBJECTIVES:

Social Skills: Students will clarify values and beliefs.

Executive Functions: Students will practice zest by showing enthusiasm for the mind-mapping activity. They will process the concept of gratitude while thinking about their values.

MATERIALS NEEDED:

- Paper
- Pencils
- 1 large, white poster board or piece of butcher paper (use 8 ½"x11" or 9"x12" if you have students work in pairs)
- Markers, paints, colored pencils, crayons
- "Mind Map" example
- Poster of Boys Town social skill, "Clarifying Values and Beliefs"

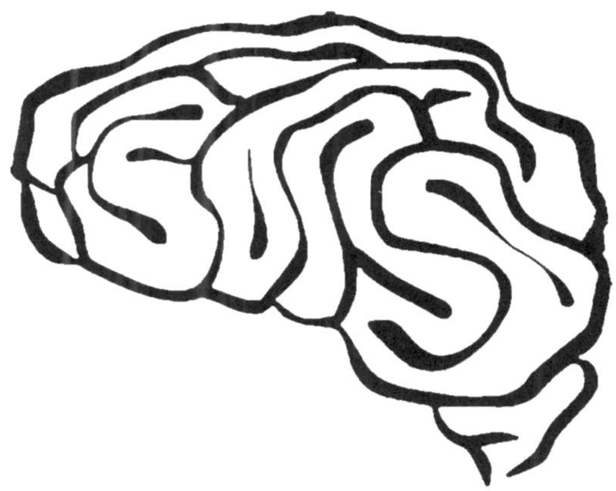

TEACHER INSTRUCTIONS:

1. Prior to this lesson, hang a large, white piece of poster board or piece of butcher paper in the room. Title it "Our Values."

2. To begin the lesson, have the students list on a piece of paper the top 7 to 10 most important things in their lives. If they think about what they are thankful for, they can build on that to identify their values. Remind them that these should be what they value the most. Ask them to be specific (e.g., saying "My dad" is not very specific, but saying "My dad because he spends time playing with me" is).

3. Next, direct the students to list on the same piece of paper the top 7 to 10 things they feel are most important to their city or state. In other words, what do they think their community values the most?

4. Finally, ask the students to list on the same paper the top 7 to 10 items they feel are most valuable to our country.

5. Once the lists are completed, have students work as a group to transfer some of the values on their lists to the poster board (or butcher paper) in order to create a **mind map**. (See the following description; a mind map example is included at the end of this activity and on the CD.)

6. Ask students to compare and contrast the values within the three categories. Follow up with questions such as:

   a. Were the three categories completely different?
   b. Were there any similarities? If so, why do you think that is?
   c. Why would an individual's values be different from our nation's value?
   d. Why would your personal values vary from those of your peers, even though you are very similar?

7. Finally, ask the students to explain the relationship between values and self-esteem. (Possible answers: Values are our moral compass. They give us a set of guidelines for our life. When our values align with those around us, then our self-esteem is affirmed. If I value what society values – hard work, helping others, etc. – then I can feel a higher sense of self-worth because I am aligned with my culture. **Values and beliefs affect our behaviors.)**

8. Ask students if there is any value or belief they want to work on. Go through the steps of **clarifying values and beliefs**:

   a. Decide which values/beliefs are appropriate and inappropriate.
   b. Choose a value/belief and determine how it could affect someone else.
   c. Identify anything you might want to change about the value/belief.
   d. Identify anything you might not want to change about the value/belief.
   e. Picture the type of person you want to be and how this might affect others.

TIPS

Compare and contrast your students' mind maps with what you can find online.

FLIPPED CLASSROOM:

Assign students to research the purpose of mind maps. Bring an example to class.

ADDITIONAL RESOURCES:

Online mind-mapping illustrations and information; mission statements of cities, states, and countries, which often give clues about values.

Sample Mind Map for This Exercise

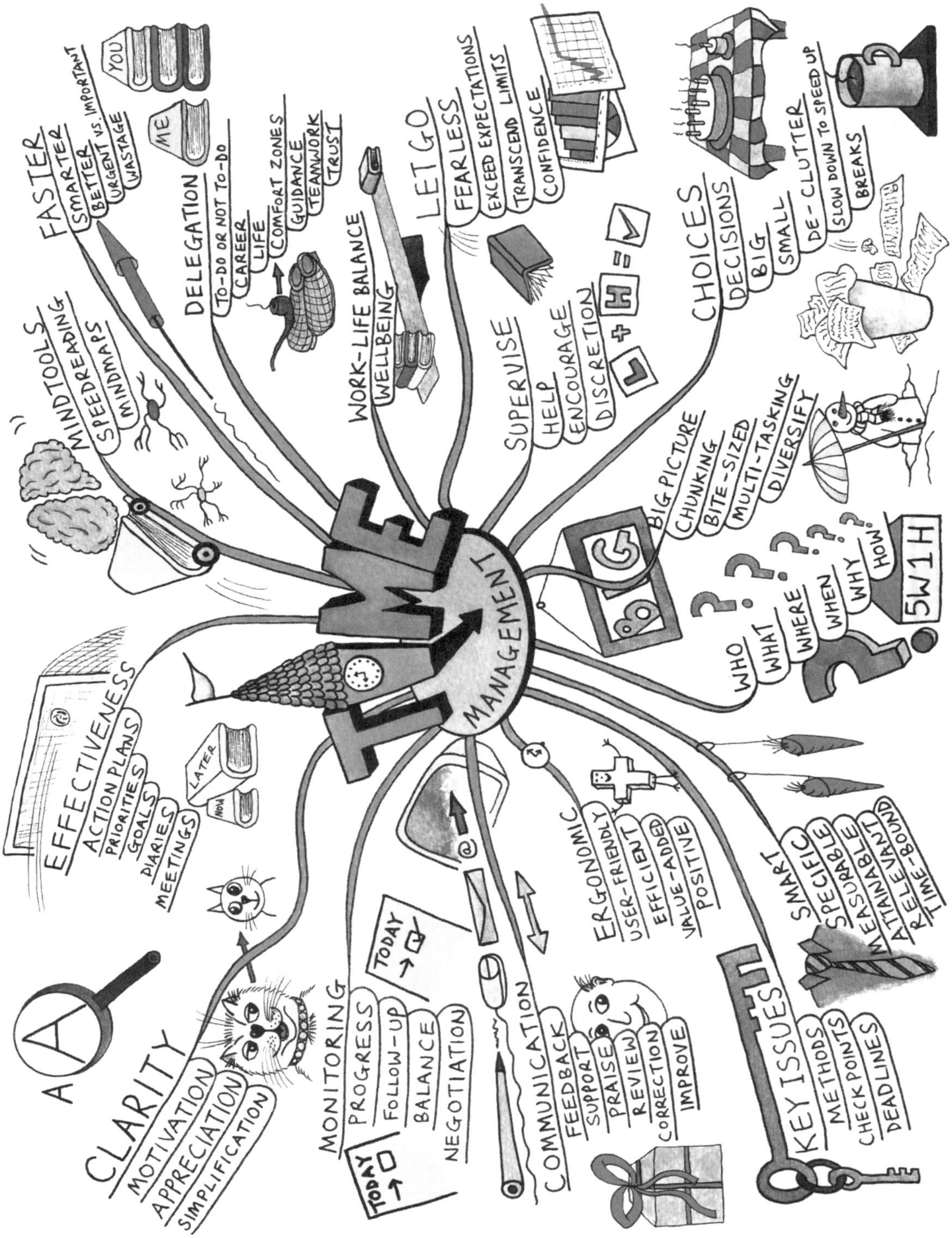

To Teach Another

OBJECTIVES:

Social Skills: Students will strive to be appropriate role models through the messages they write. They will also produce good quality work.

Executive Functions: Students will write down ways they are displaying better social intelligence when using social media.

MATERIALS NEEDED:

- Twitter or Instagram Board (This can be a long piece of butcher paper displayed somewhere in the room. Choose a width that can go through a laminator and a surface that allows students to write messages and erase them so they can post different messages at various times.)
- Vis a Vis Markers
- Paper
- Pencils
- "What's Your Handle?" sheet
- Poster of the Boys Town social skill, "Being an Appropriate Role Model"
- Poster of the Boys Town social skill, "Doing Good Quality Work"

TEACHER NOTE:

To follow the theme of self-esteem and culture, this lesson is designed to be a culminating activity for the students where they can take what they have learned and help someone else understand how their self-esteem can be influenced and shaped by the values of our culture.

TEACHER INSTRUCTIONS:

1. Explain to students that they are going to take what they have learned about social media and digital communication devices and their relationship to self-esteem, and send a message to other students, friends, or family members. Students can use either an Instagram or Twitter message, or another form of electronic messaging.

2. Tell students their messages must be 140 characters or fewer (and maybe even fewer than that on some media forms). The point is to have them write a concise and inspirational message that conveys their thoughts on self-esteem and social media and digital communication devices. Let students know they can add a picture to their messages if they like.

3. Discuss with students how this is an opportunity for them to **be appropriate role models for others**. To do this, they should:

    a. Identify a situation that requires you to be a role model.
    b. Engage in positive interactions with adults and peers.
    c. Refrain from using inappropriate language, sexual behavior, delinquency, bullying, etc.
    d. Correct peer behavior in a positive, constructive way.
    e. Remember, inappropriate role-modeling can negatively affect others.

4. You can have students post their messages either to their accounts on their devices, or on Twitter Board or Instagram Board you set up in the room.

    If you use the Board, explain to students that it will function like a Twitter or Instagram account. They will be posting their tag, photos, or messages to the paper. Have them use Twitter and Instagram language and symbols. Also ask them to use an ID name on the Board so you can track their messages weekly or bi-weekly without other students knowing who wrote a specific message. To set up this process, have students come to your desk and sign the "What's Your Handle?" sheet so you can accurately identify student comments.

    Once the Board is completed, it can be displayed in other classrooms, in hallways or common areas, or in your classroom as a visual reminder of how self-esteem can be influenced by social media and digital devices.

5. Emphasize the importance of **doing good quality work** and how it sends an impactful message to others that could potentially affect their self-esteem in a positive way. The steps are:

a. Know the exact expectations.
b. Get the tools for the job.
c. Begin working with focus and continue until the task is completed.
d. Examine your work and correct any deficiencies.

TIPS

Have students post messages weekly or bi-weekly in order for them to have the greatest impact. Remember to have students also post some messages on the "Class Interest Board."

HANDOUT

What's Your Handle?

DIRECTIONS: Write your name, your class period/block, and the social media handle you will be using for class posts.

First/Last Name	Class Period/ Block	Social Media Handle Used for Class Posts

SECTION 4

Protecting Our Self-Esteem

Understanding who we are and what we want to become are important facets in protecting our self-esteem. We not only need to guard our self-esteem with others, but also need to shield our self-esteem from our own negative thoughts and beliefs. Looking at ourselves and our abilities through a positive lens will help us achieve higher, healthier self-esteem. Setting good, healthy lifestyle habits will help us feel better about ourselves, too. Setting boundaries against the negative influences in our lives will help us develop our esteem in a more productive, successful manner. These lessons are good reminders for all of us, but are especially crucial for the adolescent student to understand and practice during these delicate years.

The lessons in this section include:

Who's in Your Circle?

OBJECTIVES:

Social Skills: Students will identify and practice setting a personal boundary.

Executive Functions: By exploring and establishing boundaries, students will exercise social intelligence and self-control.

MATERIALS NEEDED:

- Pictures of boundaries
- "Who's in Your Circle?" worksheet
- Pictures of various types of boundaries and boundary scenarios
- Poster of the Boys Town social skill, "Setting Appropriate Personal Boundaries"
- Paper
- Pencils

TEACHER NOTE:

Boundaries are tied to trust. When we trust someone explicitly, we tend to have loose, open boundaries. When someone affects us negatively, then setting solid boundaries will help to protect our self-esteem. We take control and develop more integrity and respect for our own values when we set boundaries with other people. It is a good idea to have limits with other people in all areas of our life. This leads to a more secure self-esteem.

TEACHER INSTRUCTIONS:

1. Ask students for examples of boundaries.

2. Explore the definition of "boundaries" with the students. Show pictures of various types of boundaries. The class might have several definitions, but make sure they ultimately get to an understanding that a boundary is something that protects us.

3. Ask students what a "personal boundary" is. (Possible answers: Wikipedia states that "personal boundaries are guidelines, rules, or limits that a person creates to identify for themselves what

are reasonable, safe, permissible ways for other people to behave around him or her and how they will respond when someone steps outside those limits." Merriam Webster states that boundaries are "limits that define acceptable behavior.")

4. Hand out the "Who's in Your Circle?" worksheets and have students fill out each circle according to the people in their life. See the example at the end of the activity.

TEACHER NOTE:

Sensitive issues may arise with some students. Be prepared to show compassion and support, and direct students to additional support as necessary.

5. Based on their "Who's in Your Circle?" worksheets, have students write a Personal Boundary Statement. These might resemble a School Mission Statement. Each student should write at least one, but encourage them to write more if they desire. When **setting a boundary** using the circle method, one should:

    a. Imagine that each circle represents a boundary.
    b. Picture the people you encounter in one of the circles, depending on how personally close they are to you.
    c. Share personal information only with those in your closest circle.
    d. Touch others only in appropriate ways. Respect others' boundaries.

6. Ask students what happens to our relationships when we don't respect each other's boundaries? (Possible answer: Relationships can become stressful and unhealthy.) Ask them if not respecting boundaries is worth this consequence.

7. Display the boundary scenarios or pass them out to the class.

8. Role-play different scenarios where students can practice responding to someone who is not respecting their boundaries. Explain to students that some people are not aware of others' boundaries and some might choose to ignore them so it is good to have a plan for those types of situations. (See the following scenarios.)

BOUNDARY SCENARIOS:

- Pat is Mike's best friend but has lied to him more than once. (No trust/disrespect)
- Someone continually invades your personal space. (Disrespect)
- George only likes Sally as a friend but Sally wants to be his girlfriend. (Respect issue)
- Milenka keeps getting texts from her boyfriend asking where she is and who's she with. It's becoming annoying and makes her a little nervous. (Trust issues, jealousy, controlling behavior, could lead to abuse)
- Someone is threatening to hurt you. (Bullying/abusive)
- Your friend treats you differently when other people are around. (Doesn't respect your feelings)
- Girls/Boys in the class make fun of me. (Abusive)
- I like hanging out with my good friend but she always insists we do what she wants and she always pays. (Unbalanced power in the relationship)

NOTE: *During role-plays, emphasize that students should always tell a trusted adult when a situation makes them uncomfortable.*

TIPS

Personal boundaries could potentially be a sensitive subject for some students based on past experiences. Remember to "Pin" some boundary statements to the "Class Interest Board."

FLIPPED CLASSROOM SUGGESTIONS:

Ask students to Tweet the question, "What is a boundary?" and document the responses they receive. Before class begins, ask students to write a definition of a regular boundary and a personal boundary. Discuss the meanings in class and continue with the lesson.

ADDITIONAL RESOURCES:

Search the Internet for images of boundaries to share.

NAME:______________________________________

DATE:____________________

ACTIVITY

Who's in Your Circle?

DIRECTIONS: In each boundary circle, list the names of people, or groups of people who are in your life. Your name should be on the center, and then decide who is closest to you and they would go in the next circle, and so on. Next, each circle has 2 breaks in it. This space has been left open to write in a boundary you might have with that group of people. (For example: not share secrets with acquaintances.)

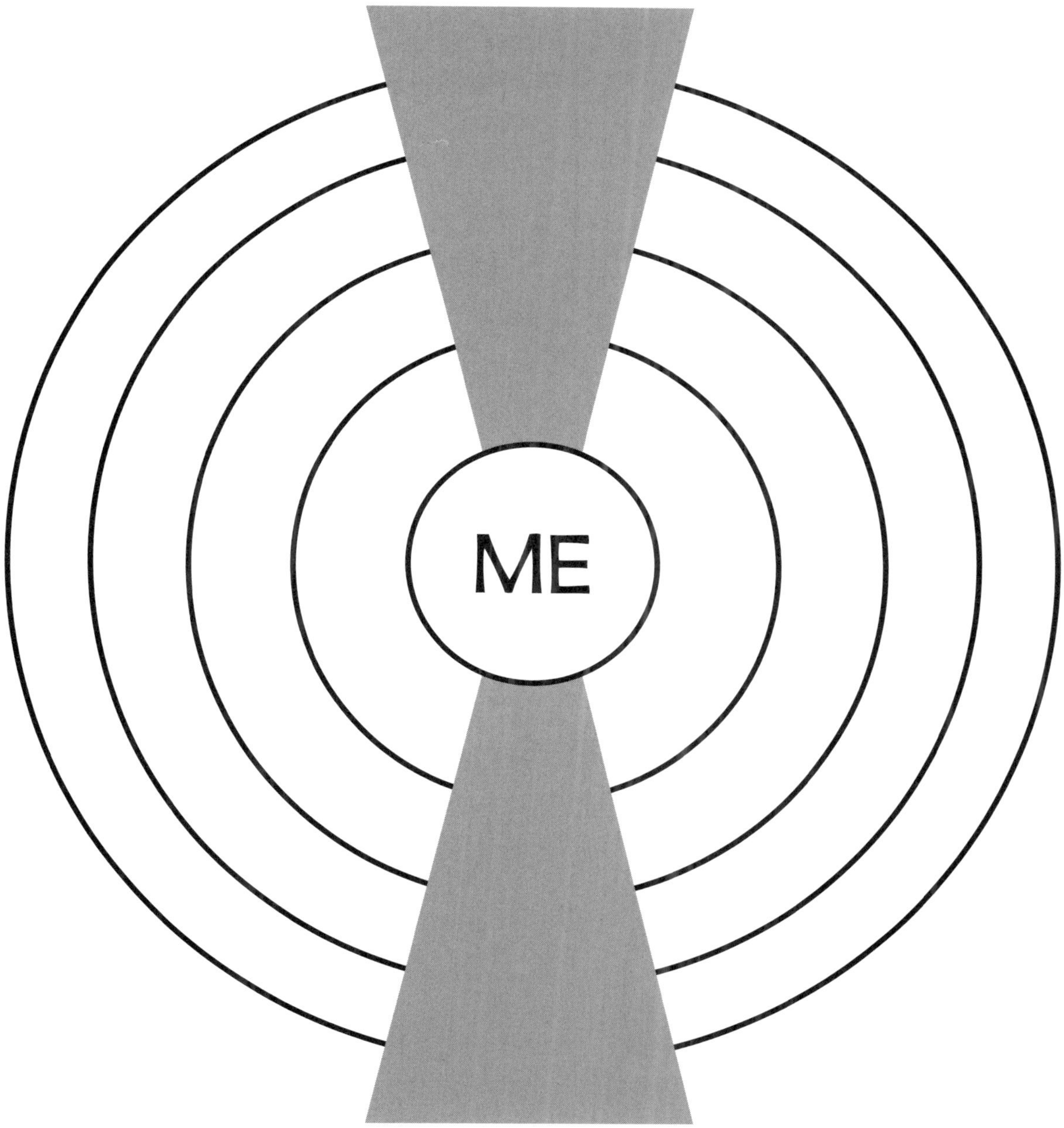

Stop the Negative Self-Talk!

OBJECTIVES:

Social Skills: Students will practice making positive self-statements and stopping negative or harmful thoughts. They will also construct positive statements about others.

Executive Functions: Students will practice optimism by believing effort (positive) will improve their future.

MATERIALS NEEDED:

- Compliment Jar (any jar will work)
- Little slips of paper for compliments
- Pens
- Composition notebooks or notepads
- Pencils
- Poster of the Boys Town social skill, "Stopping Negative or Harmful Thoughts"
- Poster of the Boys Town social skill, "Making Positive Self-Statements"
- Poster of the Boys Town social skill, "Making Positive Statements about Others"

TEACHER NOTE:

Get rid of negative thoughts and set yourself up to succeed. Thinking positive thoughts can boost self-esteem.

TEACHER INSTRUCTIONS:

1. Have students use a composition notebook or some kind of notepad to record what their self-esteem is like every day for a week. Ask them to record things such as any negative or positive thoughts they had, any negative or positive self-talk, if they tried anything new and were successful or felt defeated at anything, etc.

   The more detailed students are, the more successful the activity will be, so be sure to emphasize the importance of consciously evaluating their self-esteem every day.

TIPS

It works best to allow 10-15 minutes of class time each day for students to record their observations.

2. At the end of the week, ask students to analyze their notes. Have them circle in their notebooks any negative self-talk, thoughts, or defeats they experienced and recorded.

3. Teach students the skill of **stopping negative or harmful thoughts**:

   a. Identify the negative or repetitive thoughts you wish to avoid.
   b. When they occur, always say to yourself, "Stop!"
   c. Immediately visualize a relaxing thought or say a more positive statement.
   d. Reward yourself for using strategies to stop your negative thoughts.

4. Teach students to go a step further by **replacing the negative or harmful thought with a positive statement:**

   a. Make a positive statement about an actual occurrence or accomplishment.
   b. Don't lie or exaggerate. Be honest!
   c. Say to yourself, "I'm proud of…" or "I think I did well or better at...."
   d. Remember not to brag or put others down.

5. Discuss skill steps for these two social skills with students as appropriate.

6. Have students practice these skills by reviewing their journals, and turning the negative thoughts, self-talk, and actions into positive statements, thoughts, or perseverance.

For example, if a student had negative thoughts like, "I felt really stupid saying that in front of those girls," he or she could **CHOOSE** to say, "That was a little embarrassing. But I can laugh at myself, and if those girls don't like it, then they may not be the friends for me."

7. During the week, start using a Compliment Jar. Explain that while anyone can add a compliment about another person to the jar, each student will be assigned one classmate about whom they can write a compliment. (This ensures that every class member receives at least one compliment.) Try to steer students away from complimenting possessions or looks and toward statements that deal with character.

8. Teach students the skill of **making positive statements about others**:

    a. Try to notice or find out positive things about them.
    b. Praise a specific trait, ability, or accomplishment.
    c. Avoid saying anything that would invalidate your compliment, such as "It's about time!"

9. At the end of the week, review the compliments that have been placed in the Compliment Jar and read one for each student. Make sure you read equal numbers (i.e., if each student has two, you can read two).

I Am the Greatest!

OBJECTIVES:

Social Skills: Students will formulate ways to alter their thoughts and the environment to a more positive state.

Executive Functions: Students will generate optimism by thinking in positive ways.

MATERIALS NEEDED:

- Video clip from a movie or YouTube that shows someone persevering (Example: "The Greatest," a YouTube video by Kenny Rogers)
- Colored paper for mounting pictures
- Paper
- Pencils
- A digital picture of each student (provided by students)
- Access to computer
- Poster of Boys Town social skill, "Altering One's Environment"

TEACHER INSTRUCTIONS:

1. Show students the perseverance video clip.

2. Have students write down the response of the video's main character to failure (e.g., he or she kept trying again).

   Example: "The Greatest" by Kenny Rogers (Little boy trying to hit a baseball) (Possible answer: The boy says, "I'm the greatest pitcher in the world!" He struck himself out. The boy was focusing on finding the positive instead of allowing the negative to defeat him.)

3. Ask students to write down the response the video's main character might have had if he or she had low self-esteem.

4. Compare and contrast the two responses. Ask students:

    a. How does having high self-esteem help us? (Possible answer: We move on and don't dwell on the negative.)
    b. How does having low self-esteem hurt us? (Possible answer: We dwell on our mistakes, faults, and weaknesses, making it hard to stay positive.)
    c. Are the two different responses realistic?

5. Instruct students to think of a scenario from the past week where they failed at something and had negative thoughts. Ask them to write down how they could handle that situation in a more positive way in the future, while still being realistic. This will help to improve their self-esteem. Recognizing the difference between negative and positive thoughts helps to **alter one's environment**. Encourage the students to:

    a. Identify situations in which you encounter difficulty.
    b. Look for ways to change parts of the situation.
    c. Make appropriate changes to improve your self-esteem, behavior, and performance.

    Discuss the skill steps with students, as appropriate.

6. Have students download their digital pictures to a photo-editing program and open them. Some schools have Photoshop, but if your school does not, there are several free programs online. Here are a few you might try: www.gimp.org, http://pixlr.com, www.picmonkey.com, www.getpaint.net, Adobe Express Editor, or any other current program.

7. Have students create two new photos of themselves by digitally altering their photos (using Photoshop) to show themselves performing a task or saying something two ways, one negative and one positive.

8. Have students print their two new pictures, mount them on the colored paper, and label them "Negative Thoughts" and "Positive Thoughts," respectively. At the bottom of both, have students write, "I Have a Choice!"

9. Ask the students the following questions:

    a. Are you going to be good at everything?
    b. Were your parents and grandparents good at everything?
    c. Do you still love them?

Remind students that they don't have to be the best at everything. Help them understand they are still worthy and loveable even if they are not the best at something, and that it's more important to feel good about themselves while working on a few things at a time. Ask students to change their negatives into positives!

TELL THEM:

Remember, don't worry about being the greatest in the world (or school). Just be the greatest YOU, you can be!

TIPS

There are several video versions of "The Greatest." Choose the one you prefer.

FLIPPED CLASSROOM:

Ask students to view the YouTube video of "The Greatest" by Kenny Rogers before coming to class.

ADDITIONAL RESOURCES:

Instructions on how to Photoshop a picture. If your school does not have Photoshop, there are other free online photo-editing sites.

SECTION 5

Putting Yourself Out There!

In the following lessons, students will have the opportunity to practice "Putting Themselves Out There." The goal is to introduce students to new and unfamiliar tasks and encourage them to enjoy the process of trying something new. The ability to learn and laugh at oneself is an important facet in developing better self-esteem. When we feel "WE CAN," our self-esteem surges forward in a positive direction.

When we possess higher self-esteem, we are more likely to help others. We are not afraid of another person being successful because we are secure in who we are. When we value ourselves, we send positive messages to others about the value they have. This, in turn, promotes a healthier, more successful community and society.

Lessons in this section include:

- **Put Yourself Out There!**
- **Be Your Own Superhero!**
- **Smash It!**
- **A Message to Others**

Put Yourself Out There!

OBJECTIVES:

Social Skills: Students will be willing to take risks and try new tasks. The ability to laugh at oneself will be promoted.

Executive Functions: Students will demonstrate zest and curiosity by actively participating in the new activities.

MATERIALS NEEDED:

- 7 stations of activities (supplies are dependent upon the activities chosen)
- "Putting Myself Out There!" worksheet
- Poster of the Boys Town social skill, "Trying New Tasks"
- Poster of the Boys Town social skill, "Laughing at Oneself"

TEACHER NOTE:

Some experts say self-esteem can be learned and improved upon. Paul Tough states that, "Self-esteem can be learned, practiced, and strengthened." One way to boost confidence and improve self-esteem is to try new activities or tasks. It is okay to struggle with a new task or activity. A person doesn't need to achieve or succeed in everything he or she tries. It's more about exploring and putting oneself out there in unfamiliar territory. This is what improves confidence and self-worth.

TEACHER INSTRUCTIONS:

1. Select approximately seven activities for students to try. These could be things like language tapes, a really hard game, a new type of computer coding, sewing, a new technology application, a different kind of physical activity or exercise, some goofy type of feat, or solving difficult riddles or problems. Choose tasks that are a good fit for your students.

2. Prior to class, set up seven stations where students can explore these different activities and tasks.

3. Remind students that when they are **trying a new task**, they should:

    a. Identify what the task actually is.
    b. Think of all the steps of the new task.
    c. Breathe deeply and try your best.
    d. Ask for help or feedback if the task is difficult.

    Discuss the skill steps with students, as appropriate.

4. Have students pick three or four stations to rotate through. If time allows, you could have them complete all seven activities or tasks. Encourage the students to have fun with the tasks they are trying and to **laugh at themselves**:

    a. Identify the situation that's going to cause you some possible embarrassment or discomfort.
    b. Look for the humor.
    c. Be willing to laugh at your mistakes.

    Discuss why being able to laugh at oneself is beneficial. (Possible answer: makes others more comfortable; shows healthy self-esteem; shows willingness to have fun.)

5. After all the students have tried the tasks and activities, ask them how this relates to self-esteem. (Possible answer: Trying new tasks and activities helps build confidence, thus improving self-esteem. Being able to laugh at oneself also helps promote better self-esteem by allowing a person to make mistakes and not get upset about it.)

6. Have students complete the "Putting Myself Out There!" worksheet, which instructs students to pick one new activity or task they will try outside of class. Have students ask an adult to initial the worksheet after they have tried the new activity or task. Set a due date for the assignment.

TIPS Plan for safety.

ADDITIONAL RESOURCES:

Search for new tasks students can try.

NAME:______________________________________

DATE:____________________

ACTIVITY

Putting Myself Out There!

DIRECTIONS: *Pick a new activity or task you will try. Fill out this form. When you have accomplished your goal, get an adult signature to serve as a witness, then, return the form to your teacher*

New activity or task I will try:

Date Accomplished: ________________________

Signature: ________________________________

Be Your Own Superhero!

OBJECTIVES:

Social Skills: Students will work independently and produce good quality work.

Executive Functions: Students will display grit and zest by working enthusiastically with focus.

MATERIALS NEEDED:

- Access to computers
- Paper (optional)
- Craft supplies (optional)
- Poster of "Superhero Traits/ Adaptations List"
- "Define My Superhero" worksheet
- Images of several real-life and fictional heroes
- A digital photo of each student (provided by students)
- Poster of the Boys Town social skill, "Working Independently"
- Poster of the Boys Town social skill, "Doing Good Quality Work"

TEACHER NOTE:

People look up to heroes. They represent the good in humans. They touch and influence lives. They inspire us to overcome our adversities. Heroes WIN at life. By thinking positive and being realistic, students can develop their own traits and become their own Superhero! Each student CAN represent good. Each student CAN influence lives! Each student CAN overcome difficulties! Each student CAN WIN at life!

TEACHER INSTRUCTIONS:

1. Prior to starting this lesson, ask students to send a digital photo of themselves to their school email address. They will use the photo for this assignment.

2. Have students download their photo to a photo-editing program and open their photo. Some schools have Photoshop, but if your school does not, there are several free programs online. Here are a few you might try: www.gimp.org, http://pixlr.com, www.picmonkey.com, www.getpaint.net, Adobe Express Editor, or any other current program.

3. Before beginning, ask students to define the term "Superhero." Discuss student responses. (Merriam Webster defines superhero as "a fictitious hero having extraordinary or superhuman powers.")

4. Show students the images of several fictitious and real-life heroes.

5. Explain to students that they will use their photos to turn themselves into a Superhero in the photo-editing program.

6. Instruct students to include certain self-esteem characteristics they feel they possess as they construct their Superhero. (You also could have students construct Superhero bodies out of craft supplies and then put a photo of the student's face on the Superhero's body.)

7. Ask students to identify the traits they would like to possess 10 years from now and have them adapt their Superhero to include those traits. (If thinking of other traits is difficult, then let the students select a few from your "Superhero Traits/Adaptations List.")

8. On a project like this, it is important to **work independently** and produce good quality work. Teach students to:

    a. Start on the task promptly without procrastinating.
    b. Remain on the task until it is completed
    c. Check back with the person who assigned the task.

9. Remind students that to **do good quality work**, they should:

    a. Know the exact expectations.
    b. Get the tools for the job.
    c. Begin working with focus and continue until the task is completed.
    d. Examine your work and correct any deficiencies.

Discuss skill steps with students as appropriate.

10. Hand out the "Define My Superhero" worksheet and have students complete it. Discuss the students' answers as a class.

11. (Optional) Celebrate self-esteem by throwing a class party. Have each student dress like their favorite Superhero.

TIPS

Encourage students to steer away from looks and athletic ability when identifying their Superhero characteristics and focus more on character, values, and self-esteem traits.

FLIPPED CLASSROOM:

Have students research Superheroes and identify their powers and characteristics. Ask them to bring a list of at least five physical, five mental, and five self-esteem Superhero traits to class.

NAME:____________________

DATE:__________

ACTIVITY

Define My Superhero

DIRECTIONS: A Superhero typically originates as an ordinary person. Consider the questions below to define your Superhero.

1. What kind of problems would he or she face? ____________________

____

2. What does your character think about the world? ____________________

____

3. What does your character do to keep his identity safe? ____________________

____

4. What does your character do to keep his self-esteem safe? ____________________

____

5. Will your character's superpowers affect the lives of ordinary people in any way? How?

____

____

6. Will your character be able to solve problems in new ways? ____________________

____

____

7. What is holding you back from becoming your own Superhero? ____________________

____

HANDOUT

Superhero Traits/ Adaptations List

Here are some suggested ways Superheroes can transform:

good communication
energetic, changeable
adventurous
honest
rugged
resourceful
laughs at self
confident
powerful
courageous
mind power
creative
charming
helpful
speed
strength
can fly

can climb walls
exceptional leaping
teleports
elasticity
invisibility
changes colors
tail spikes
uses sensors to detect heat
night vision
stores oxygen in cells so doesn't have to breathe continuously
floats

Smash It!

OBJECTIVES:

Social Skills: Students will assess their own abilities and accomplishments while concentrating on their project.

Executive Functions: Students will work independently with grit and self-control.

MATERIALS NEEDED:

- Scrapbook paper or construction paper of various colors
- Glue sticks
- Three-hole punch
- Book rings
- File folders or sturdy cardstock (e.g., blank chipboard)
- A homemade Smash Book
- Craft supplies for decorating pages
- Poster of the Boys Town social skill, "Concentrating on a Task"
- Poster of the Boys Town social skill, "Assessing Own Abilities"

TEACHER NOTE:

If you are part of the scrapbooking world, you will be familiar with Smash Books. They are a type of fancy journal that is an easy way to document what is going on in your life. You can use any theme you want when making a Smash Book. If you are not familiar with them, just do an online search and you will find many examples and instructions. Use your creativity and imagination!

TEACHER INSTRUCTIONS:

1. Prior to doing this lesson in class, create a Smash Book you can show students as an example. Or, you can have students find examples online (search for "Smash Books").

2. Before beginning the activity, explain to students that this project will take time to complete and will require them to **concentrate on their work**. They will need to:

    a. Begin work promptly.
    b. Focus on the task.
    c. Ignore distractions or interruptions.
    d. Remain on task until finished.

3. Hand out the "Smash Book Instructions" handout to students and walk them through the following instructions for creating their own Smash Books. Feel free to adapt these instructions or use other design materials as you see fit!

    a. Ask your teacher for permission to view examples of Smash Books online so you can get ideas.
    b. Create a cover using a sturdier type of cardstock.
    c. Mod Podge scrapbooking paper to the cover's surface and decorate it according to your tastes. (Make this unique to you! Use glitter, colors, and anything you like from the available materials.)
    d. Create interior pages out of a sturdy cardstock or file folders cut to size. Include approximately 18 inside pages.

TEACHER NOTE:

You may adjust this number, depending on the assignment goals, length, and available materials.

    e. Mod Podge scrapbooking paper, digital images, or other types of paper to the surface of the pages. (You can decorate the pages anyway you choose using Washi Tape, pockets, envelopes, pocket tabs, glitter, sequins, little objects, etc.)
    f. Use a three-hole punch and book rings to connect the covers and pages.

4. Explain to students that they will use their Smash Books as a Self-Esteem Success Book in which they keep track of and document events that promote higher self-esteem or lead to higher self-esteem in their lives (especially during the current school year).

    For instance, maybe a student scores a C- or D+ on a test that he studied for, but this is an improvement over the F's he has received in the past when he did not study. He could include the test and write a sentence or two about how this increased his self-esteem.

    Or maybe a student volunteered to help someone or did something new or different that was difficult for her. One of her pages could be about that event. The goal is to get this student to see ways she can build higher self-esteem, thus promoting more success and happiness in life.

5. As students consider the types of events they want to record in their Smash Books, help them learn to **assess their own abilities and accomplishments**. To do so, a student should:

   a. Make a list of your strengths and weaknesses.
   b. List situations when you have been successful.
   c. Think about future activities where you could use these skills.

6. To get started, have the students include five pages in their Smash Books with the following titles and ask them to fill these in over the course of the project. They may keep adding to these pages as they think of things they feel should be on them.

   a. "I can…"
   b. "I am…"
   c. "I will…"
   d. "I like…"
   e. "I value…"

TEACHER NOTE:

This could be used as an ongoing project and the Smash Books could be shared at parent-teacher conferences. Have students include 10 to 12 different pages on how they improved their self-esteem and the five "I" pages.

TIPS: Provide ample time for this project. Having a sample Smash Book would be ideal.

FLIPPED CLASSROOM:

Assign students to find an image of a Smash Book and bring it to class. Discuss its purpose as a class. Then continue with lesson plan.

ADDITIONAL RESOURCES:

Online images and instructions for making Smash Books.

Smash Book Instructions

DIRECTIONS: Use the steps below as a guide to create your own Smash Book!

1. Ask your teacher for permission to view examples of Smash Books online so you can get ideas.

2. Create a cover using a sturdier type of cardstock.

3. Mod Podge scrapbooking paper to the cover's surface and decorate it according to your tastes. (Make this unique to you! Use glitter, colors, and anything you like from the available materials.)

4. Create interior pages out of a sturdy cardstock or file folders cut to size. Include approximately 18 inside pages.

5. Mod Podge scrapbooking paper, digital images, or other types of paper to the surface of the pages. (You can decorate the pages anyway you choose using Washi Tape, pockets, envelopes, pocket tabs, glitter, sequins, little objects, etc.)

6. Use a three-hole punch and book rings to connect the covers and pages.

7. Label five interior pages:
    a. "I can…"
    b. "I am…"
    c. "I will…"
    d. "I like…"
    e. "I value…"

8. Follow your teacher's instructions to create and manage this as an ongoing project.

In the scrapbooking world there is something known as Smash books:

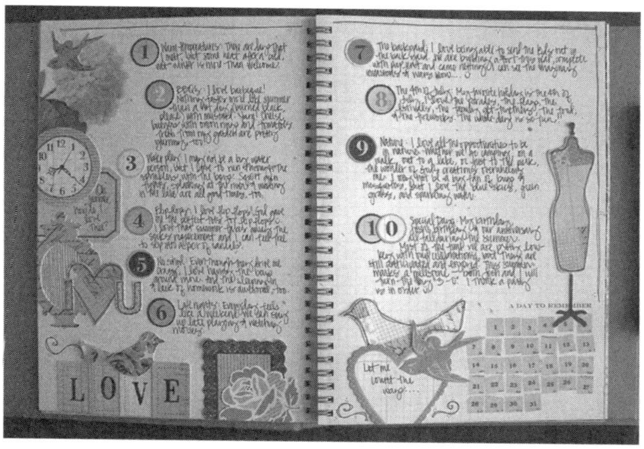

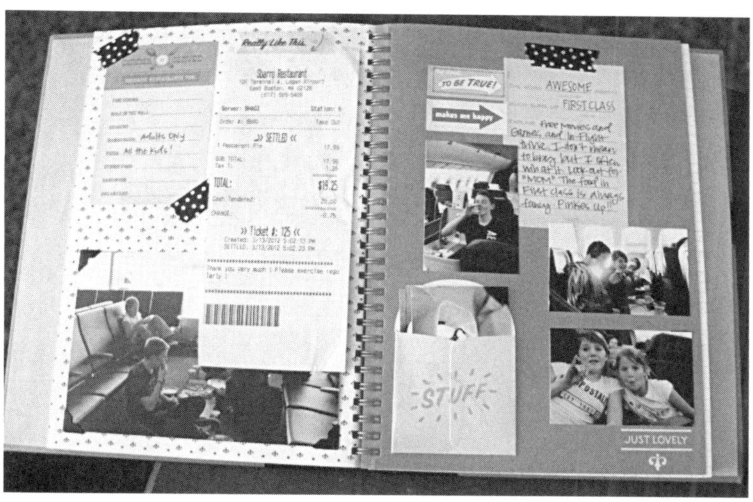

A Message to Others

OBJECTIVES:

Social Skills: Students will create a self-esteem visual message by carefully selecting the appropriate words to use for the greatest impact.

Executive Functions: Students will practice self-control by allowing others to contribute and promptly beginning their work.

MATERIALS NEEDED:

- Whiteboard or chalkboard
- Examples of Animotos, 15-second Instagrams, and 6-second Vines (these are different programs used in making short, impactful, digital video messages)
- Paper
- Pencils
- Access to computers
- Poster of the Boys Town social skill, "Choosing Appropriate Words to Say"

TEACHER INSTRUCTIONS:

1. Explain to students that having good self-esteem makes it easier for them to reach out to others and help them cultivate higher self-esteem. Ask students to list five things they have learned about improving their self-esteem.

2. Write the class's list on the board.

3. Divide the class into groups of two or three. Students also could work individually.

4. Explain to students that they will be using either the class list on the board or a group or individual list to compose an *Inner Message about Having Healthy, Positive Self-Esteem.*

5. Explain that words are powerful and have the ability to influence people for good or for ill. Emphasize the importance of **choosing the appropriate words** for the message they are sending. To do this:

    a. Look at the situation around you.
    b. Know the meaning of the words you will use.
    c. Avoid using words that will offend others.
    d. Avoid using slang, profanity, or words with a sexual meaning.
    e. Decide what thought you want to put into words then say it.

6. Have each group (or student) spend time composing their *Inner Message about Having Healthy, Positive Self-Esteem.*

7. After the groups have composed their self-esteem messages and have checked for word appropriateness, ask them to produce their message in the form of an Animoto, a 15-second Instagram, or a 6-second Vine message.

    Show examples of each media form to the students in case some students are not familiar with these. You may also use another program of your choice. Music can be added to these programs.

8. Share the messages with the school in a commons area or post them to your class or school website for others to view.

TIPS

Emphasize that the messages should be brief but impactful.

FLIPPED CLASSROOM:

Assign students to view an Animoto, 15-second Instagram, and 6-second Vine before coming to class. Ask them to choose the one they will use to produce their message, and to write and bring a rough draft of the message to the next class.

APPENDIX

Skills and Their Steps

SECTION 1: *DEFINING SELF-ESTEEM*

Talking With Others

- Look at the person.
- Use a pleasant voice.
- Include others by asking questions.
- Don't interrupt when someone else is talking.

Staying On Task

- Look at the task and think about the steps needed to complete it.
- Focus all your attention on the task.
- Stop working only when given permission by the adult who gave you the task.
- Ignore distractions and interruptions by others.

Assessing Own Abilities

- Make a list of your strengths and weaknesses.
- List examples of when you have been successful or have had problems.
- Think about future activities where you could use your abilities.

Identifying Own Feelings

- Examine how you are currently feeling.
- List and think about how your feelings change with different situations and experiences.
- Think about how you could monitor your feelings and emotions when situations occur.
- Correctly identify and label your feelings.
- List your feelings.

Making Positive Self-Statements

- Make a positive statement about an actual occurrence or accomplishment.
- Don't lie or exaggerate. Be honest!
- Say to yourself, "I'm proud of…" or "I think I did well or better at…."
- Remember not to brag or put others down.

Analyzing Tasks

- Ask questions to clarify the assignment, if necessary.
- List the steps of the task.
- Put the steps in order.
- Begin completing the steps in order.

SECTION 2: *HOW WE GOT HERE*

Contributing to Discussions

- Look at the people who are talking.
- Wait for a point when no one is talking.
- Make a short, appropriate comment that relates to the topic.
- Choose words that will not be offensive or confusing to others.
- Give others a chance to speak.

Displaying Effort

- Remain on task and work diligently.
- Do your best to accomplish tasks to criteria.
- Inform others of your efforts if appropriate.

Assessing Own Abilities

See steps in Section 1

Setting Goals

- Decide on an overall value and lifestyle desire.
- Identify the resources you need to meet these.
- List the steps you need to take to meet your goal.
- Establish short- and long-term goals that will help you meet these steps.

SECTION 3: *THE WORLD AROUND US*

Analyzing Social Situations

- Think about the people you've encountered.
- Look at the situation.
- Assess the behaviors of others.
- Choose the behavior or reaction that seems most appropriate.

Persevering on Tasks and Projects

- Know what must be done.
- Get started promptly without procrastinating.
- Remain on task until you are finished.
- Deal appropriately with any frustrations.

Self-Monitoring and Reflection

- Think about the behaviors you are engaging in and your feelings about this.
- Label these behaviors and feelings.
- Determine whether they are appropriate.
- Identify alternate behaviors or skills that would be more productive.

Setting Appropriate Personal Boundaries

- Imagine a series of circles radiating out from you. Each circle represents a boundary.
- Picture people you know or encounter in various circles, according to the relationship you have with them.
- Disclose personal information only to those in your closest circle.
- Touch others only in ways that are appropriate to your relationship with them and to your boundaries.

Cooperating with Others

- Discuss the task with others.
- Know what to do.
- Give and accept constructive criticism with peers.
- Share resources.
- Praise peers' efforts.

Gathering Information

- Know the topic by researching it further.
- Ask for help if needed.
- Assemble the necessary materials and data.
- Write down and organize the main information.

Clarifying Values and Beliefs

- Decide which values/beliefs are appropriate and inappropriate.
- Choose a value/belief and determine how it could affect someone else.
- Identify anything you might want to change about the value/belief.
- Identify anything you might not want to change about the value/belief.
- Picture the type of person you want to be and how this might affect others.

Being an Appropriate Role Model

- Identify a situation that requires you to be a role model.
- Engage in positive interactions with adults and peers.
- Refrain from using inappropriate language, sexual behavior, delinquency, bullying, etc.
- Correct peer behavior in a positive, constructive way.
- Remember, inappropriate role-modeling can negatively affect others.

Doing Good Quality Work

- Know the exact expectations.
- Get the tools for the job.
- Begin working with focus and continue until the task is completed.
- Examine your work and correct any deficiencies.

SECTION 4: *PROTECTING OUR SELF-ESTEEM*

Setting a Personal Boundary

See steps in Section 4

Stopping Negative or Harmful Thoughts

- Identify the negative or repetitive thought you wish to avoid.
- When it occurs, always say to yourself, "Stop!"
- Immediately visualize a relaxing thought or say a more positive statement.
- Reward yourself for using strategies to stop your negative thoughts.

Making Positive Self-Statements

See steps in Section 1

Making Positive Statements about Others

- Try to notice or find out positive things about another person.
- Praise a specific trait, ability, or accomplishment.
- Avoid saying anything that would invalidate your compliment such as "It's about time!"

Altering One's Environment

- Identify situations in which you encounter difficulty.
- Look for ways to change parts of the situation.
- Make appropriate changes to improve your self-esteem, behavior, and performance.

SECTION 5: *PUTTING YOURSELF OUT THERE!*

Trying New Tasks

- Identify what the task actually is.
- Think of all the steps of the new task.
- Breathe deeply and try your best.
- Ask for help or feedback if the task is difficult.

Laughing at Oneself

- Identify the situation that's going to cause you some possible embarrassment or discomfort.
- Look for the humor in the situation.
- Be willing to laugh at your mistakes.

Working Independently

- Start on the task promptly without procrastinating.
- Remain on the task until it is completed
- Check back with the person who assigned the task.

Doing Good Quality Work

See steps in Section 4

Concentrating On a Task

- Begin work promptly.
- Focus on the task.
- Ignore distractions or interruptions.

Assessing Own Abilities

See steps in Section 1

Choosing Appropriate Words to Say

- Look at the situation around you.
- Know the meaning of the words you will use.
- Avoid using words that will offend others.
- Avoid using slang, profanity, or words with a sexual meaning.
- Decide what thought you want to put into words, then say it.

BIBLIOGRAPHY

Author Unknown Quote. https://www.mindbloom.com/apps/inspiration/detail/quote/5d828c6f-1d3f-4fbc-b3fc-7835a585a54c/. Retrieved March 27, 2015.

The Story on Self-Esteem. http://kidshealth.org/kid/feeling/emotion/self_esteem.html. Retrieved March 27, 2015.

Tough, Paul. Self-esteem quote. https://www.goodreads.com/author/quotes/1186184.Paul_Tough. Retrieved March 27, 2015.

Various definitions. http://www.merriam-webster.com/. Retrieved March 27, 2015.

Zentic, Zane. *Does a Hamburger Really Have to Be Round?* Story.